Resolving Patient Complaints ▼

A Step-by-Step Guide to Effective Service Recovery

Second Edition

Liz Osborne, M.S.

JONES AND BARTLETT PUBLISHERS

Sudbury, Massachusetts

BOSTON   TORONTO   LONDON   SINGAPORE

World Headquarters
Jones and Bartlett Publishers
40 Tall Pine Drive
Sudbury, MA 01776
978-443-5000
info@jbpub.com
www.jbpub.com

Jones and Bartlett Publishers Canada
2406 Nikanna Road
Mississauga, ON L5C 2W6
CANADA

Jones and Bartlett Publishers International
Barb House, Barb Mews
London W6 7PA
UK

This publication is designed to provide accurate and authoritative information in regard to the Subject Matter covered. It is sold with the understanding that the publisher is not engaged in rendering legal, accounting, or other professional service. If legal advice or other expert assistance is required, the services of a competent professional person should be sought. *(From a Declaration of Principles jointly adopted by a Committee of the American Bar Association and a Committee of Publishers and Associations.)*

Library of Congress Cataloging-in-Publication Data

Osborne, Liz.
   Resolving patient complaints : a step-by-step guide to effective service recovery / Liz Osborne.—2nd ed.
      p. cm.
   Previous ed. published: Gaithersburg, Md. : Aspen, 1995.
   Includes bibliographical references and index.
   ISBN 0-7637-2622-2
      1. Health facilities—Complaints against. 2. Managed care plans (Medical care)—Administration. 3. Medical personnel and patient. 4. Patient satisfaction. I. Title

RA965.6.O83 2003
659.2'936211—dc21

                                                                    2003047438

Publisher: Michael Brown
Production Manager: Amy Rose
Associate Editor: Chambers Moore
Production Assistant: Jenny L. McIsaac
Senior Marketing Manager: Alisha Weisman
Associate Marketing Manager: Joy Stark-Vancs
Manufacturing Buyer: Amy Bacus
Cover Design: Philip Regan
Interior Design: Dartmouth Publishing, Inc.
Composition: Dartmouth Publishing, Inc.
Printing and Binding: Courier Stoughton
Cover Printing: Courier Stoughton

Printed in the United States of America
07 06 05 04 03   10 9 8 7 6 5 4 3 2 1

This book is dedicated to my father, Walter Hesse, in memoriam.

Acknowledgments

I would like to thank Ken Bayne, Empire Health Services, for his contribution to the chapter on dealing with potentially violent patients, and Doug Martin, Evergreen Community Home Health and Hospice, for his help with the home health staff scripting. And, as always, thank you to my former colleagues, Donna Davison-Smith, Kristine Leander, Ellen Martin, and LeAna Osterman for their unflagging support and friendship over the years.

Contents

Acknowledgments iv

Introduction.. ix

Chapter 1 Patient Complaints Are Important.. **1**

   Why Patient Complaints Are Important 3

   Service Recovery—What Is It? 5

   Service Recovery—Why It Is Important.. 5

Chapter 2 Service Recovery.. **9**

   Service Recovery—Establishing the Procedures 10

      Identify the Most Frequent Problems 10

      Develop Options for Resolving Problems................................ 11

      Train Staff in Service Recovery Processes 12

   Service Recovery—How To Do It 14

      Customer Contact... 14

      Acknowledge the Problem 15

      Problem Solve and Respond 16

      Refer/Respond 16

      Follow Up 17

      Atonement 18

Chapter 3 Service Recovery: Additional Considerations............................. **21**

   Culpability Scale... 22

   Emotional Overlay 22

      Neutral/Blasé Blues 22

      Annoyed/Ornery Orange 23

      Victimized/Redhots... 23

   Complexity of the Issues/Depth of the Review 25

      Level 1 25

      Level 2 25

      Level 3 25

      Level 4 25

      Level 5 26

      Level 6 26

   Patient Expectation for Resolution 27

Chapter 4 Review Process for Clinical Quality-of-Care Complaints 29

Nursing and Ancillary Staff 31

Medical Staff 32

"Informal" Review Process for Level 1 through Level 4
Complaints—Blasé Blue and Ornery Orange 32

"Formal" Review Process for Level 5 and Level 6 Complaints—
Red Hots 34

Chapter 5 Correspondence with Patients 45

Initial Letters 45

Follow-Up Letters 50

Progress Report Letters 52

Billed for Copy of Patient Records 56

Hold or Suspend Billing 58

Decertification 60

Results of the Review 62

Letters for Level 1 through Level 4 Complaints 62

Letters for Level 5 and Level 6 Complaints 64

Transfer of Case to Risk Management 66

Financial Settlements 68

Chapter 6 Documenting, Tracking, and Reporting Patient Complaints 71

Documenting Complaints 72

Tracking Complaint Activity 77

Which Information to Enter into the Database 77

Reporting Complaint Activity 82

Chapter 7 Identification of Trends 85

Trending Physician Complaints 85

Trending Nonphysician Complaints 92

Chapter 8 Dealing with the Difficult Patient 93

The Annoying Patient 94

The Challenging Patient 94

Historians 94

Socially Isolated Patients 95

Head Injury Patients 95

The Overly-Involved Family 95

The Noncompliant Patient 96

The Isolated Incident 96

The Abusive Patient 97

The System Abuser 97

The Law Breaker 102

The People Abuser 106

Behavior Requiring Immediate Action 116

Appendix A Service Recovery Protocols for Medical Receptionists 121

Model 121

Medical Receptionist 123

Appointment Wait Time for Own Primary Care Practice 123

Appointment Wait Time for Specialist 125

Staff Attitude 127

Access to Own Primary Care Physician 129

Mid-Level Practitioner Appointment, not MD Appointment .. 131

Pharmacy Wait 133

Quality of Care 134

Timely Return Call from Registered Nurse 136

Telephone Access 137

Waiting Room Delay 138

Appendix B Service Recovery Protocols for Physicians 141

Model 141

Physicians 143

Waiting Room Delay 143

Quality of Care 144

Appointment with Mid-Level Practitioner 145

Noncovered Service 146

**Appendix C Service Recovery Protocols for the
Patient Representative Department 149**

Model 149

Patient Representative Department 151

Appointment Wait Time 151

Staff Attitude or Customer-Service Orientation 154

Handling of Complaints and Concerns 156

Not Active on System/New Enrollee, Denied Services 158

Mid-Level Practitioner Appointment, Not MD Appointment . 161

Quality of Care 163

Appendix D Service Recovery Protocols for Member Services Departments 167

Model 167

Marketing Department/Business Office 169

Appointment Wait Time 169

Staff Attitude or Customer Service Orientation 172

Disputed Billing 174

Co-Payments 177

Incorrect Personal Data in System 178

Insurance Enrollment Card Request 180

Lack of Complete Information about Coverage 183

Enrollment Status Dispute 186

Referral Process—Internal/External 189

Termination of Coverage 191

Appendix E Service Recovery Protocols for Home Health Agencies 195

Model 195

Clinician Late for Appointment 197

Late for Appointment 198

Quality of Care 199

Disputed Billing 200

Multiple Providers 202

Appendix F Procedure for Formal Medical Staff
Review of Quality-of-Care Complaints 205

Procedures for Review 205

Contents of Level 5 and Level 6 Medical Staff Review Packet 206

Final Letters in Level 5 and Level 6 Quality-of-Care Cases 207

Guidelines for Referring Cases to Risk Management 208

Case Files 208

Contents of Level 1 through Level 4 Case Files 209

Appendix G Subject of Complaints 211

Inquiry 213

Quality of Medical Care 214

Quality of Service 215

Policy 218

Complaint Handling 221

Abusive Patient Behavior 221

Additional Readings 223

Index 227

About the Author 233

Introduction

We all have at least one customer service nightmare we are eager to share with our companions. It doesn't matter if the incident occurred ten years ago; the memory and the emotions are as fresh as if it happened yesterday. What shifted these episodes of poor service into the nightmare category was often how the employee and supervisor handled—or did not handle—the customer's complaint.

By now, most people are immune to an indifferent sales clerk or receptionist; it happens so often we are prepared either to push for what we want or to ask to speak to a supervisor. Hiring the right people—those who care about providing good customer service—and then training them to have the product knowledge and skills they need is a major challenge for any company.

But even in a perfect world problems occur. Even the companies so highly touted as icons of exemplary service have some dissatisfied customers. Poor service takes place in retail, in hospitality, and in other service industries, and it happens in health care.

Your office or department may have the best staff to deliver care in the best and most efficient way possible. The staff has been trained in customer service skills. The billing system has been updated. The office uses the latest technology. The physicians, nurses, therapists, and aides are among the best in their field.

Still, sometimes things go wrong.

Nothing—no person, no system, no organization—can be 100% perfect. We may have implemented TQM/CQI systems in our attempt for perfection, and we may be satisfied when we come close. Suppose you have analyzed different aspects of your office and made some changes. The bills are now correct 95% of the time; the receptionist accurately schedules appointments 97% of the time; the lab test results are accurate 94% of the time. You are justifiably pleased with those results. But what does that mean over time?

Actually, even with those scores, there would still be problems. Examples from "Is 99.9% Good Enough?"* have been circulating for many years. The original article, by Natalie Gabel in the March 1991 issue of *Training* magazine, cited statistics of what happens when we are close to perfection:

- 22,000 checks will be deducted from the wrong bank accounts in the next 60 minutes;
- 1,314 phone calls will be misplaced by telecommunication services every minute;
- Two million documents will be lost by the IRS this year.

Ms. Gabel also cited some health care examples:

- 12 babies will be given to the wrong parents each day;
- 291 pacemaker operations will be performed incorrectly this year;
- 20,000 incorrect drug prescriptions will be written in the next 12 months;
- 107 incorrect medical procedures will be performed by the end of the day today.

It has been more than 10 years since this list was put together. Since then, computers have become a staple in our daily lives, increasing the volume of transactions and, thus, the number of mistakes, even while retaining 99.9% accuracy.

The business of practicing medicine is more complicated than it used to be. At all levels, providers not only diagnose and treat their patients, they also have a variety of reimbursement agreements with insurers, resulting in participation in different provider networks. Managers juggle the volume of work that five years ago was handled by two or three people, if there are middle managers left at all. Sometimes, it seems that bureaucratic layers create insurmountable barriers between the provider and the patient.

In the middle of all this, the patient arrives, sometimes bewildered by "The System," sometimes afraid, and usually with an expectation of what will happen during the appointment, the hospital stay, or the home visit. Patients bring their own view of the world, their own idiosyncracies.

The patient then encounters receptionists, nurses, physicians, and technicians, who each have their own perspectives and visions of what should occur.

In *Patient Satisfaction Pays: Quality Service for Practice Success,* Stephan Brown and his associates identified the factors that influence patients' perceptions when they are receiving medical care*:

- their prior experience with other physicians and health care organizations as well as with their current physician's office;
- what they have learned about physicians and health care from newspapers, magazines, radio, television news and network programs, the Internet, movies, books, and educational materials;
- what they have heard about their physician, as well as about other physicians, from friends, family, co-workers, and other patients;
- their current medical condition and health care needs.

So what do we do when the patient thinks things have gone wrong?

*Reprinted with permission from the March, 1991 issue of *Training* Magazine. Lakewood Publications, Minneapolis, MN. All rights reserved.

*S. Brown, et al, *Patient Satisfaction Pays: Quality Service for Practice Success.* 1993, p. 30.

Excellent customer service skills are important. But sometimes "smile training" is not enough. Sometimes the patient leaves dissatisfied with the service received. If staff do not consider resolving patient complaints to be part of their job, or do not have confidence in their own problem-solving skills, or do not have the authority to handle a problem, then most likely the patient will leave even angrier than before. To keep the problem from becoming a customer-service nightmare in the patient's eyes, the staff need to know how to respond to a patient's dissatisfaction appropriately and effectively. This is an additional skill not usually included in customer-service training programs. This book provides managers, physicians, and employees with these additional skills and tools.

First, it provides a process for patient-oriented complaint-handling, or "Service Recovery," that can be used by all staff. It shows how to identify common patient complaints about service in an office, clinic, or health care system, as well as how to involve all employees in developing fast, fair fixes to those complaints. Although this book has a managed-care focus, the basic principles can be applied in any health care setting—solo practice, large-group practice, hospital, home health or long-term care facility—just as these principles are already being applied in a wide variety of other service industries. This process works well for responding to the vast majority of the concerns patients bring to staff. The staff feel comfortable dealing with the situations because they have been given the responsibility for resolving the problem, the skills to do it well, and the information they need to do so.

Many industries implemented Total Quality Management (TQM) and Continuous Quality Improvement (CQI) programs before health care organizations adopted these principles. Both TQM and CQI provide tools for evaluating and improving delivery systems. But these processes take time. In the interim, there are patient/customers who are unhappy with a particular aspect of their care and who want a resolution to their concerns—NOW.

Both manufacturing and service industries have found that Service Recovery is cost-effective and retains customers. Although some hotels, retail stores, and financial institutions have formalized the way they respond to customer concerns, only a small percentage of health care organizations have adopted the systems described in this book. Yet the basic principles and steps for Service Recovery are probably not new to the many patient representatives and others who deal with patient/customer concerns on a daily basis. They just never stopped to analyze what often comes naturally.

In addition to the basic components of Service Recovery, this book describes one process used successfully for over 15 years to review and respond to more complex or serious complaints, especially patient concerns about quality of care. A process such as this can help an organization meet Health Care Finance Administration (HCFA) and accreditation agencies' standards for a grievance process. As a byproduct, the process can help reduce risk-management claims rates and the costs associated with professional liability issues, not to mention the emotional strain on staff when a claim is filed. The review process can actually enhance patients' satisfaction and understanding of their medical care.

Also found in this book are:

- a system for documenting patient comments and complaints in a logical, straight-forward manner, as well as a strategy for monitoring and analyzing the information documented by patient comments;
- a mechanism to change behaviors of health care providers and to improve delivery systems;

- strategies for dealing with difficult and abusive patients;
- sample scripted responses using Service Recovery protocols for some of the most common types of complaints heard by different practitioners, responses that can be used to assist staff to develop their own.

Why are these tools and processes important? Because the relationship has changed between the patient/customer and the provider. The physician no longer practices with total autonomy and control. Insurance company benefits managers review services provided by all types of practitioners and determine what will be paid for and what will be excluded from coverage. More and more patients with insurance are locked into some kind of managed care program, whether it be a staff model, a preferred provider network, a primary care network, or some other type of alliance. The patient/customer has a contractual relationship with the "Plan" to receive care and services. This means the providers must work with the patient/customer—even if that person is sometimes unreasonable or difficult.

Often patients' "difficult" attitudes or behaviors are the result of frustration at not receiving the care or service they feel they should. Most now have access to tremendous amounts of information from the Internet and various publications, and they intend to participate actively in their health care. When they do not receive the care or service they think they should, or when there is a breakdown in communication, patients may feel they are being held captive. Changing providers is not as easy as it once was, and, depending on the type of service, the patient may have few if any alternatives to choose between. It is in everyone's best interest for staff to promote a positive relationship with patients.

Everyone benefits when a staff person takes a few minutes to work with the patient/customer to identify the source or cause of the frustration, and then to resolve it. When problems are resolved quickly and fairly, patient/customers feel "heard" by the staff, have their needs met, and therefore will be loyal patients. The staff's confidence in their ability to solve problems is enhanced. The front-line staff will have the skills—and the permission—to resolve problems within the parameters set for them, handling the situations well so the patient/customer's frustration does not escalate. The staff shares in identifying solutions, which allows them to feel more involved and committed to their work.

Physicians will learn how to respond to complaints they hear without feeling defensive or ignoring the problem. The manager or administrator does not need to be called in to resolve simple problems that have escalated, freeing them to deal with other issues. There is consistency in how problems are resolved. The practice or clinic benefits from retention of patients, higher patient satisfaction ratings, and good public relations.

Accreditation organizations have included patient-complaint and grievance procedures in their credentialing criteria. For a number of years, hospitals have been required by the Joint Commission for the Accreditation of Healthcare Organizations (JCAHO) to have a mechanism for addressing patient complaints, but those mechanisms have ranged from very sophisticated patient-representative programs to an add-on function for an administrator, director of nursing services, or social worker. In 1999, HCFA added "Notice of Patients' Rights and Grievance Process" to its list of patient protection standards. The new standards apply to *all* hospitals participating in Medicare and Medicaid programs.

With evolving accreditation standards, grievance-resolution processes may need to be formalized throughout the Plan, facility, or system. Currently, most clinics and small group practices have informal arrangements among the staff to handle patient complaints. These informal methods may not meet patient needs, and regrettably staff sometimes prefer that angry patients leave the practice because they are too much trouble.

Unfortunately, these patients will share their "nightmares" with others, including insurance carriers. This could affect the ability of the solo practitioner or group practice or agency to continue as a network participant, and may ultimately impact the provider's financial viability. High patient satisfaction with complaint resolution can only benefit the provider.

For simplicity, the term "staff" is used throughout the book to refer to all employees and health care providers, including physicians. The term "organization" refers to alliances, managed care systems, multihospital/clinic systems, preferred-provider networks, agencies, group-practice clinics, and other types of linkages for providing medical care. The job title "Patient Representative" refers to the person responsible for implementation and oversight of the complaint-management program, Service Recovery, and the formal grievance process.

The basic principles found in this book are applicable to all organizations, from solo-practitioner offices to multihospital/clinic systems. How those principles are formalized and implemented depends on the organization.

There is no single way to respond to patient complaints. Many of the processes described in this book were used successfully for over 15 years by a large HMO. These procedures are one suggestion of how to approach patient complaints. You, the reader, should take these ideas and modify them to meet the needs of your organization and staff.

There are no guarantees that any problem-solving system will be successful every time. Sometimes a patient is unwilling to work with staff. Sometimes staff do not recognize the patient is unhappy until it is too late. And no one really *likes* to deal with complaints. But health care staff who have used Service Recovery report that with the right tools and processes, helping unhappy customers can be a more valuable and rewarding aspect of the services they provide.

Chapter 1

Patient Complaints Are Important

It's not what you say, but what is heard.
It's not what you show, but what is seen.
It's not what you mean, but what is understood.
Perception is reality.

—author unknown

Patient expectations have changed. Many patients are active consumers of health care, comparing quality, service, and cost. They expect the highest technical quality of care, excellent customer service, and good value for the money they pay. They are interested in alternative treatments, and they ask more questions. They spend hours researching on the Internet. They do this for themselves, for their children, and for their aging parents. They judge the quality of the care and service they receive from *their* perspective.

Patient/customers do not compare the service they receive solely with what they have received from other healthcare providers. They also compare it to the service they have received from other service industries. If hotels can serve over one thousand people at a banquet with excellent food that is consistently fresh and hot, then why does a hospital have difficulty delivering good quality meals? If Federal Express can guarantee next-day delivery of millions of packages anywhere in the country, then why are test results often delayed or lost between the lab and the physician's office?

With these changing attitudes and expectations, healthcare providers—particularly physicians—find they are no longer deified. They are increasingly viewed as professional experts who are being asked for information and opinions. Many patients are not content to be passive recipients of services. They often want some control over their treatment

1

decisions. The relationship between physician and patient is changing. It is evolving into a partnership or association in which the patient expects to participate equally in the diagnosis and treatment decision process. Increasingly, insurance benefits administrators are joining the relationship and influencing treatment option discussions.

Successful providers, clinics, hospitals, and other healthcare organizations recognize these shifts in attitude and are responding to them. There are myriad reasons why health care is "different," and cannot always be compared to other service industries. However, there are some lessons learned by these other companies that can be transposed to health care.

During the 1980s, hospitals and other healthcare organizations conducted "service excellence" or "guest relations" training for staff, reinforcing the need to "be nice" to the patient/customer.

In the late 1980s, healthcare organizations started accepting as a given that the people hired to care for patients were basically good, honest, friendly, people-oriented employees, and that management should instead look at the "systems" preventing those employees from providing excellent service on a consistent basis. Organizations began adopting Total Quality Management (TQM) or Continuous Quality Improvement (CQI) methods for improving systems. Initially, TQM and CQI were developed by W. Edwards Demming with a manufacturing focus. The goal of these improvement projects is "zero defects"[1] (the Zero Defects theory was proposed by Philip Crosby in 1961); that is, every widget, every television, every automobile that comes off the assembly line, every billing statement, every you-name-the-product will be made to the highest standards and will perform as promised by the manufacturer.

Add to this activity the pressures of cost-containment and cost-reduction on healthcare providers vis-à-vis diminished rates of reimbursement from government agencies and large insurers, and healthcare providers at all levels are feeling squeezed. It is no wonder that patients are often frustrated.

A basic reality for all types of service organizations is that quality service is not necessarily a tangible product that either does or does not work. "Service" is intangible. Customers compare their *expectation* for service with their *perception* of how well that expectation was met, and then they react to that perception. These expectations can be as varied as the customers who request the service. When this occurs in as subjective an environment as medical care, there will be differences of opinion, problems, or—simply stated—complaints.

Good service is invisible; poor service and outstanding service are conspicuous. If the customer's expectation for service is dramatically exceeded, the customer will be pleased, delighted—and very loyal. If the expectations are not met, the customer will be dissatisfied.

All people have their own individual expectations and foibles. And they interact with others who have their own sets of perceptions.

Consider the waiting room.

One patient/customer comes to the physician's office expecting to wait. She bases this on personal experience, her friends' experiences, and other sources such as frequent newspaper cartoons about waiting-room delays. Prepared to wait for the appointment, she brings some work with her and settles into a corner chair. This patient will be pleasantly surprised when she is called to go to the exam room only 10 minutes after her scheduled appointment time. This patient is delighted because the service exceeded her expectation.

Another patient arrives expecting she will be seen in the exam room by the physician at the scheduled time of her appointment. She views a sliding schedule as a sign of staff incompetence, and possibly, a deliberate attempt to irritate her. She sits in the waiting room, foot tapping and arms crossed, and is annoyed if she is not called to the exam room at the time of her appointment. This patient is dissatisfied because her expectations were not met, and she shares her dissatisfaction with everyone within earshot.

▼ Why Patient Complaints Are Important

In her book, *Customer Service Nightmares*, Nancy Friedman includes a letter from one patient who described the argument his wife had with a billing clerk over charges for the couple's premature baby. The clerk finally said that if the woman didn't want any problems, she should have had a healthy baby.[2]

Most of us gasp or cringe when we hear a story like that, and we know it happens all too often. The patient called to resolve a billing problem, and the way she was treated exacerbated her dissatisfaction. Most patients expect they will have to sort through some billing issue, but they do not expect to be treated poorly when they attempt to resolve it.

When you read this example, did it trigger a memory of your own service nightmare? Do you feel angry all over again? Do you want to share your experience with others? If so, you now understand at a visceral level why good complaint handling is important.

Every time patients come in contact with a healthcare provider or organization, they make a judgment about the quality of the care or service they received. They make this judgment when they call on the telephone for advice or to schedule an appointment, try to find a parking place, check in for the appointment, sit in the waiting room, and with every other contact, up to and including when they pay the bill.

These little incidents are called "moments of truth." Taken individually, patients may not think much about the minor inconveniences. However, if they experience problems with each and every one of these encounters, or have one significant negative experience, they will begin to question whether to continue receiving medical services from that organization or facility.

For the most part, patients assume they are receiving high-quality medical care. Nevertheless, when small service problems arise, patients become more critical, even to the point of challenging the technical competence of their providers. Drs. Leonard Berry, A. Parasuraman, and Valarie Zeithaml, service researchers, identified five attributes consumers use to evaluate the quality of the service they receive*:

- **Reliability** (ability to perform the promised service dependably and accurately);
- **Responsiveness** (willingness to help customers and provide prompt service);
- **Assurance**, which includes:
  - *competence* (possession of the required skills and knowledge to perform the service);
  - *courtesy* (politeness, respect, consideration, and friendliness of contact personnel);

---

*Reprinted with permission of The Free Press, a Division of Simon & Schuster Adult Publishing Group, from *Delivering Quality Service: Balancing Customer Perceptions and Expectations* by Valarie A. Zeithaml, A. Parasuraman, Leonard L. Berry. Copyright © 1990 by The Free Press.

- *credibility* (trustworthiness, believability, honesty of the service provider);
- *security* (freedom from danger, risk, or doubt);
- **Empathy**, which includes:
  - *access* (approachability and ease of contact);
  - *communication* (keeping customers informed in language they can understand and listening to them);
  - *understanding the customer* (making the effort to know customers and their needs);
- **Tangibles** (appearance of physical facilities, equipment, personnel, and communication materials).

These same five attributes can be found in a high-quality, customer-oriented problem-solving, or "Service Recovery," process. When customers do not find these attributes, they go somewhere else for service.

Contractual relationships between hospitals, physicians, other providers, and insurers have already changed the way healthcare services are delivered. Patient/customers choose an insurance plan, often some form of preferred-provider or managed care plan, to meet their healthcare needs, and are usually "locked in" to that organization for one year, before having an opportunity to change coverage. This is similar to most large employers' "open enrollment" periods for changing insurance coverage. The benefits will be basically the same for each of the plans.

The difference will be in the patient/customer's perception of quality and value. Some of the perception of quality and value will come from the "report cards" that compare organizations' clinical and patient-satisfaction ratings for a variety of services. Most of the patient/customer's perceptions, however, will be based on personal experiences and hearsay.

Consumer research indicates that each person who has a negative experience will tell up to 20 people about that experience. The staff of large managed-care organizations find that patient/customers do not talk to their friends and acquaintances about the problems they had with "Dr. Brown"; instead, they refer to problems they encountered with "Hilltop Health Plan."

If members of the plan who have experienced a negative "moment of truth" begin sharing that incident with others, an organization's community reputation can be devastated, regardless of the overall competence of the care and service. The organizations that are successful in retaining existing enrollees and attracting new ones will be the organizations that:

- take care of the individual patient/customer who experienced the problem
- identify system problems
- correct the system so the problem does not reoccur

One of the best ways to enhance patient/customer perceptions of the organization's quality and service is to implement a service-recovery process that includes all staff.

▼ Service Recovery—What Is It?

When a service breakdown occurs, the staff have an opportunity to work with the upset patient to "recover" from that breakdown and retain a loyal customer. If staff efforts to resolve the complaint compound the problem, the organization usually loses the customer. But if the problem is resolved, and resolved well, that customer may be even more loyal than a customer who has never encountered a service problem.

Although manufacturing companies use TQM/CQI methods to achieve "zero defects," service industries must acknowledge that there will be problems and focus their efforts on processes aimed at "zero defections" (a phrase created by Bain and Company).[3]" Service Recovery is a planned, organizational approach to actively solicit and then resolve patient/customer concerns quickly, fairly, and in a manner that makes the offended patient/customer feel satisfied with the *process,* as well as the *outcome.*

Simply stated, Service Recovery is a way to anticipate service problems, save potential service disasters, and pay attention to the patient/customer's feelings while fixing the problem.

First, take care of the customer (feelings), then take care of the problem. Service leaders have done just that by identifying their customers' most frequent concerns, and establishing prescribed ways to deal with them. Nordstrom employees are taught to take any merchandise back; Marriott front-desk employees know exactly what to do if a reservation error occurs; and Disneyland staff have guidelines for refunding guests' money because of inclement weather. These companies know how to take care of their customers, and those customers do not hesitate to pay more for the perceived extra value. Although the industries are different, the service principles remain the same and can be applied to healthcare services.

▼ Service Recovery—Why It Is Important

People expect value for their money. When a problem occurs, the person who takes care of the patient/customer and then takes care of the problem will generate loyalty from that patient/customer.

There is economic value in keeping customers. Marketing studies have shown that it costs at least five times more to attract a new customer than to retain a current one. Think of the time, money, and effort that goes into

- marketing efforts to recruit new patient/customers
- setting up new accounts and files, and requesting previous medical records
- meeting pent-up demand for services
- getting to know the patient

Consider the difference between losing and replacing 20% of a primary-care practice or clinic's patient/customer group each year, as opposed to losing and replacing 5% of the patient/customer group during that same time period. A 20% rate is the equivalent of a complete patient/customer turnover every five years. For a net annual growth of 5%, the practice must recruit new patients to replace the 20% it lost, plus an additional 5%. This rate of "churn" can make the difference between a smoothly run office with a stable patient/customer practice, and an office that both staff and patients feel is always in chaos.

The Technical Assistance Research Project (TARP) is widely respected for the extensive consumer research it conducted for the U.S. Office of Consumer Affairs; TARP found that regardless of the type of business involved, the primary reason people stopped using a particular company was because they had encountered a problem or unpleasant surprise in a transaction with the company. The existence of a problem would result in a 20% decrease in average loyalty,* and, if it was not rectified, up to a 60% decrease.*

Other studies show that the primary reasons why patients changed physicians were perceptions that the physician was not spending enough time with them during an office visit, was unfriendly, or did not answer questions—all interpersonal interaction issues.

Satisfied customers are those who have their needs and expectations met. When a problem occurs, the healthcare professionals who treat the patient/customer well, while fixing the problems quickly and fairly, will have higher patient satisfaction ratings than those who do not. This service edge can translate into increased retention of patients as well as attracting increased numbers of new patients.

Nobody likes to deal with an unhappy or angry patient/customer. When a patient expresses dissatisfaction with some aspect of service, the natural tendency is to feel defensive and to want to blame the problem on someone else (or the patient), or to ignore the complaint and brush the patient off.

This response can actually exacerbate the problem, making the patient/customer even angrier—angry enough to change physicians, transfer to a different healthcare provider, switch insurance coverage—angry enough to tell any friend or relation who will listen and share the outrage, angry enough to sue, and, unfortunately, angry enough to become violent.

On the other hand, problems that are responded to quickly in a caring, personalized manner not only resolve the problem, but can also create a bond between the patient/customer and the employee, physician, healthcare provider, or insurance carrier. The "delighted" patient/customer will share this experience with friends and relations.

The Technical Assistance Research Program (TARP) also researched how consumers respond when they are dissatisfied with services; TARP found that unhappy customers, especially those who complained and were dissatisfied with the way the complaints were handled (and with the resolution) created losses for a business that affected it financially in the long term.* These included loss of the individual customer, loss of that customer's repeat business, and loss of image or reputation when the customer shared the poor experience. At least twice as many persons were told about a bad experience as a good experience. In some industries, as many as six times as many heard about a bad experience.

On the other hand, a customer satisfied with the way a complaint was handled more likely resulted in long-term profits for repeat business, referrals to other potential customers, reduced regulatory and litigation costs, and reduced costs of recruiting and setting up new customers.*

Consumer research has identified six criteria for complaint handling that meets the customer's psychological needs for feeling valued by the institution or department:

*J.A. Goodman, The Nature of Customer Satisfaction (paper presented at the meeting of the National Quality Forum IV, 1988, revised 1993).

- it is easy to complain—staff on site can handle the problem and are readily available so that the customer is not transferred to another person or department more than once;
- one person assumes responsibility for investigating and resolving the problem;
- the resolution is fair—the customer is given options, the resolution is reasonable, and staff follow through as promised;
- the process is fast—the staff react to the problem and resolve it quickly, preferably within one day;
- staff provide clear, consistent information, and all questions are answered to the patient/customer's satisfaction;
- the patient/customer is acknowledged as being important—staff does not brush the patient/customer off: staff listens to the problem, and the patient/customer's perspective is accepted as valid and taken seriously.

Sometimes patient/customers expect that the first person they talk to will handle the concern; other times they want to talk to someone "with authority" or someone not directly involved with the problem.

A mechanism for reporting and discussing their concerns gives patients an alternative to hiring an attorney and filing a claim to resolve their grievances. Given the costs of mediation and litigation, if even the filing for court action is avoided, Risk Management should be a visible supporter of such a program. It also helps the organization meet regulatory and accreditation standards.

Perhaps the most important reason for a Service Recovery program, however, is the well-being and satisfaction of the patient. The patient and family need to feel confident in the technical quality of care provided and be satisfied with the quality of service. Usually a justified basis for concern with the quality of clinical care arises in only a small percentage of patient complaints. Most dissatisfaction can be attributed to patients feeling "brushed off" by the physician, or to problems with communication and understanding of the issues surrounding their treatment.

Health care is more complicated than the banking, hotel, and entertainment industries. For one thing, the patient/customers are more emotionally charged, often with a high fear factor. And the ever-changing reimbursement arrangements create a complexity of problems that did not exist with fee-for-service medicine.

But one truth remains constant. It is more cost effective to keep existing patient/customers than to replace them. A reputation for high technical quality of care may attract patient/customers to a particular physician, hospital, or organization. However, it is the way the patient/customer is treated, the "high touch" factor, that determines the patient/customer's loyalty.

Businesses such as Nordstrom and Marriott have shown that people will gladly pay more if they believe they are receiving better or higher value. Handling patient complaints well is cost effective. The patient who feels heard by the staff of the clinic, the hospital, or the organization will be a satisfied customer—and will remain with the practice. Not only will Service Recovery increase patient/customer loyalty, it will also assist staff in identifying recurring system problems that can be addressed with TQM/CQI methods. Service Recovery helps improve the overall quality of service in the office, clinic, hospital, and organization, which can only lead to greater patient/customer satisfaction.

NOTES

1. P.B. Crosby, *Quality Without Tears: The Art of Hassle-Free Management* (New York: North American Library, 1984), 76.

2. N. Friedman, *Customer Service Nightmares: 100 Tales of the Worst Experiences Possible, and How They Could Have Been Fixed* (Menlo Park, CA: Crisp Publications, 1998), 28.

3. "Zero Defections" is a copyright of Bain and Company.

Chapter 2

Service Recovery

The fact that we are a multi-regional, multi-divisional, multi-functional, multi-site, and multi-product organization is not the customer's problem.

—Ronald Kubinski
Manager, Corporate Quality, 3M

Most customers expect problems with service. They also expect the problem to be resolved after they report it to the organization. How well the staff respond to patient/customers who are unhappy will affect their decision to stay with the practice or managed-care plan, or to leave. Service Recovery means that a service breakdown has occurred, and that staff correct the problem to the customer's satisfaction. The Service Recovery process can help any organization achieve the goal of retaining patients as loyal customers, or "zero defections."[1]

Technical Assistance Research Programs (TARP) identified that customers leave when their complaints are not responded to well (see list of titles in Additional Readings). Ron Zemke and Chip Bell of Performance Research Associates, Inc., went one step further. They identified the specific components that should be included in a complaint-handling, or Service Recovery process, and have written extensively on the applicability of these processes in service industries such as hotels and banking. Although many of the issues raised by patients in health care are different from problems in hotels or banking, the principles and processes for responding to those issues are the same.

One of the reasons Service Recovery works is that problems are anticipated and planned for in advance. This increases the staff's confidence and ability to respond to patient/customer needs, and gives them parameters for resolving complaints.

9

▼ Service Recovery—Establishing the Procedures

This process involves several steps:

- Identify the most frequent problems reported by patient/customers;
- Develop options for resolving the problems;
- Train staff in Service Recovery processes and given "solution spaces" that specify boundaries for decision making.

Identify the Most Frequent Problems

If you ask staff to talk about patient complaints, it is only human nature for them to become defensive. A better way to start the discussion is to share a personal customer service nightmare experience (not healthcare-related) and solicit similar stories from them. After they have shared their experiences, look for the common theme. Usually it is how poorly the complaint was handled that made the incidents so memorable. After this introduction, staff should be more receptive to talking about the patient complaints they hear.

If staff are asked what patient/customers complain about most often, they will probably identify five or six issues without pausing to think. However, it helps to support the staff's perceptions with data. For a two-week period, have staff track the number and type of complaints they receive. This can be done with

- Tick marks on printed lists of the complaints staff identified as most common;
- Cards to jot down notes regarding what the complaint was about, how it was resolved, and problems encountered when trying to resolve it (Figure 2-1);
- A combination of tick marks and cards.

At the end of two weeks, sort and tally the information between the most common or *frequent* complaints, and the most *important* complaints. They may not be the same.

The most frequent complaints may be about hospital food or clinic parking. But these are not issues that usually result in patient/customers choosing to change physicians or insurance carrier.

The important complaints are those that involve issues that keep patient/customers loyal to the physician, hospital, or organization, or that drive them away. In health care, these "loyalty factors" can involve the following areas:

- perceived technical competence of providers
- interpersonal relationship with all staff
- access to appointments or other services
- perceived coordination of care between different departments and providers
- complaint handling

Suppose the tally shows a high number of complaints about parking, and a somewhat smaller number of complaints about appointment availability. To increase patient/customer loyalty, staff should address appointment availability first, because patient/customers will decide where to receive services based on that issue.

Figure 2-1 Quick Form

MADRONA MEDICAL CENTER	
☐ Telephone access — lines busy, put on hold	Date:_____
☐ Wait for scheduled appointment	Time:_____
☐ Parking	Initials:_____
☐ Waiting room wait time	
☐ Exam room wait time	
☐ Staff attitude	
☐ Quality of care	
☐ Timely call back — nurse	
☐ Timely call back — physician	
☐ Billing — charges too high or incorrect, insurance coverage dispute (circle one)	
☐ Lab	
☐ Answering service	
☐ Other (specify) _____	

Details:_____

_____

How did you resolve it:_____

_____

_____

What would have helped/what more did you need to resolve it: _____

_____

Similarly, if the hospital shows a high rate of dissatisfaction with food, and a small but steady level of complaints about nurse attitudes, it is better to focus on the attitude problem first.

Complaints are an opportunity for staff (and the organization) to show patient/customers that they are valued as individuals and that their satisfaction is important. If a patient/customer takes the time to express a concern and the staff does nothing—or, worse yet, the staff treats the patient/customer poorly—the aggrieved patient/customer will feel undervalued and will go elsewhere for service.

Develop Options for Resolving Problems

Once the most frequent problems and those associated with loyalty factors are identified, the next step is to develop options for resolving them.

If the problem is a "system issue," then a permanent solution can be developed and implemented using the appropriate TQM/CQI processes. However, this may take time. While the problem is being studied and a system change is developed, or if the problem is not conducive to TQM/CQI processes, other options for taking care of the patient/customer need to be considered.

Developing options should be a team process, something everyone in the office—physician, nurse, receptionist, and any other staff—is involved in. For example, if the receptionist hears frequent complaints from patient/customers about the number of days or weeks they have to wait for a routine physical exam appointment, then the physician and nurse should be involved in discussing options for setting aside more time for those appointments. Perhaps the decision is made to squeeze the unhappy patient into a different time slot (take care of the person), and the physician decides to run some Saturday clinics just for routine physicals to decrease the wait time to a more acceptable length of time (the system fix).

In the hospital, the nurse hears frequent complaints about the discharge process. She responds to the patient who is having the problem (takes care of the individual problem) and works as part of a team to improve the process (the system fix).

Appendices A through E provide models for responding to the individual complaints for different departments or staff within the facility or organization. These samples include possible options for resolving the problem. They can be considered as examples for staff when developing their own Service Recovery protocols.

Train Staff in Service Recovery Processes

Once the team develops the specific protocols for handling the most frequent complaints and those involving loyalty factors, all staff should be trained, coached, and assigned a readily available mentor (usually the patient representative or designated manager or administrator) for developing their Service Recovery skills. Some staff may want the six Service Recovery steps printed on a note card taped next to the telephone to help them remember the process. Others find that a notebook or "shingle cards" that include scripting for various types of complaints are a helpful reference.

Part of the training should include a technique recommended by Ron Zemke and his associates called "Solution Spaces" (Figure 2-2). They have also been called "Decision Zones." These are the parameters for staff that define their scope of decision-making authority when resolving patient/customer concerns. For a number of years, there has been considerable discussion about empowering employees. Using these "spaces" or "zones" helps accomplish that goal.

The staff person in solution space 1 is authorized to make decisions up to a certain point; the staff person in solution space 2 is authorized to make the same decisions at 1's level, plus a higher level of decisions. Staff person 3 has the widest range of decision-making authority.

The zone approach defines the "safe zone," the "low-risk zone," and the "high-risk" zone. All employees have the authority to make decisions in the "safe zone"; an employee should consult with a supervisor in the "low-risk zone"; and a supervisor must be involved in "high-risk zone" issues.*

For example, if the patient/customer has waited more than 30 minutes after the scheduled time of an appointment, the receptionist (space 1) may be authorized to waive an appointment copayment but may not be authorized to waive other fees. The recep-

---

* Reprinted with permission of The Free Press, a Division of Simon & Schuster Adult Publishing Group, from *On Great Service: A Framework for Action* by Leonard L. Berry. Copyright © 1995 by Leonard L. Berry.

Figure 2-2 Solution Spaces

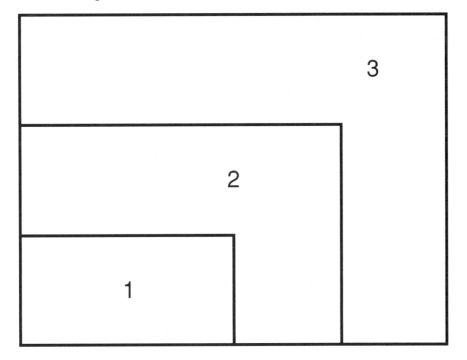

tionist (space 1) may not be authorized to schedule a "nonurgent" patient in an "urgent" appointment slot, but the registered nurse (space 2) does have the authority to do so.

In the hospital, a patient may complain that the room is too cold. The nurse's aide or patient-care technician (space 1) would give the patient extra blankets and turn up the heat for that room, but the nurse (space 2) must be involved in the decision to move the patient to a different room, and the manager or patient representative (space 3) could decide if the bill should be adjusted.

Whatever the boundaries are, they need to be clear to the staff. Once the agreements are reached, management must support the decisions made, and not return to second-guess every staff decision.

If staff are authorized to write off charges, they must be assigned a budget code or given the necessary funds. Otherwise, resolving complaints that impact their department's or another department's budget only creates conflict between the staff responsible for complaint handling and those responsible for the budget, a no-win barrier to a quality process.

When responding to patient concerns about service, physicians need to differentiate between the "medical model" and the "service recovery model." When a patient presents a list of symptoms to the physician, the physician generally follows the medical model for arriving at a diagnosis and a treatment plan. However, the medical model does not adapt well to patient complaints about service or about medical care. The Service Recovery model is a different way of addressing the patient's problem—is a different thought process—and works better in these situations because the patient has a *different expectation* for the response.

▼ Service Recovery—How To Do It

Once the most common, and important, service complaints have been identified and the solution spaces or decision zones have been clarified, the staff can be taught how to use Service Recovery. Service Recovery gives staff a step-by-step process, or a way to identify and respond to these different expectations and perceptions of quality service.

Zemke broke the components of a quality Service Recovery process into six steps:

- customer contact
- acknowledge the problem
- problem solve and respond
- refer/respond
- follow-up
- atonement

The following sections will explain each of these steps. Examples of Service Recovery scripting for specific complaints for different departments or staff can be found in Appendices A through E.

All staff, from receptionists to physicians, should learn how to use Service Recovery skills. These basic steps can take only a few minutes for simple problems or can be expanded to respond to more complex issues.

Customer Contact

On a busy day, it may be difficult for staff to give each patient/customer individualized attention, to stay completely focused on that person. One way for staff to focus on providing that personal attention to each and every patient is to recognize that in only a few minutes a bond of trust and confidence must be forged, information shared, decisions and agreements made. Another method is to practice mentally blocking everything else out, and then pay attention to the patient/customer's body language as well as her words.

Solicit the concern. Identifying that the patient/customer is dissatisfied is not always easy. Some studies show that half to three quarters of people who are dissatisfied with service never say a word. They simply leave and do not return.

Before the patient/customer leaves the office, clinic, or facility, at least one, if not two, members of the staff should actually ask the patient/customer about the visit:

"How was your visit today?"

"Do you have any questions or concerns I can help you with?"

"Is there anything else we can do for you today?"

A deskcard may serve as a helpful reminder to staff. If the patient/customer is upset or bothered about something, these questions—if asked in a sincere, caring manner with eye contact—should elicit a response.

Listen attentively. Use body language that indicates interest and concern when the patient/customer does express dissatisfaction with some aspect of service or care. Continue eye contact, nod to show understanding, keep arms uncrossed, and, if appropriate, take notes. Over the telephone, give the caller an opportunity to speak without interruption, but interspersed with comments, such as, "I see," or "uh-huh," to let the caller know someone is still listening.

Ask questions. After the patient/customer has explained the problem, the staff person should ask questions to clarify the patient/customer's perspective of the problem and to obtain specific details about who, what, where, when, why, and how.

Empathize. A single statement by the staff person that recognizes the patient/customer's perspective will do much to gain that person's trust and loyalty. Empathy is not feeling sorry for someone. Empathy is showing understanding and sensitivity to the situation; a recognition that the person is upset, regardless of the reason or the staff's perception of the validity of the person's reason. An empathetic statement provides a humanistic touch that can calm an upset person, and defuse anger, for example:

"I understand that you are frustrated by this."

"I'm glad you let me know how important this is to you."

What does the patient/customer want? Sometimes patient/customers will tell staff what they want as a resolution. In other cases, the staff must ask what patient/customers expect or what they would like done to resolve the problem. Knowing what they want helps in two ways. First, it lets patient/customers know they are important. Second, it provides a framework for staff to resolve the problem. The patient/customer who wants an apology is easily satisfied; the patient/customer who wants the nurse fired for being rude will probably need more staff time and attention to satisfy. In either case, knowing the patient/customers' expectations for resolution, their perception of what is a "fair fix," will help staff respond appropriately. This can, however, be difficult with very angry patient/customers. In some cases, it is better to offer some options for the patient to choose from, rather than ask what they want.

Acknowledge the Problem

After learning what the problem is, the staff's next step is to acknowledge the patient/customer's *feelings,* or their reaction to the problem, regardless of how trivial it may seem to the staff. If the incident is important enough for the patient/customer to be upset, it is important enough for staff to respond. Before the problem can be resolved, the patient/customer must be taken care of.

Apologize for the inconvenience/not meeting their expectations. Some people believe that apologizing is an admission of guilt. It is not. Rather, it is simply a validation of the patient/customer's feelings and emotional reaction to the situation. The apology is for the patient/customer's perception of inconvenience, for the perception of being wronged, for example:

"I'm sorry this wasn't what you were expecting."

"I'm sorry the information wasn't clear to you."

Repeat the problem. Restate the problem by paraphrasing to ensure clarity and understanding of what is upsetting the patient/customer.

Patient/Customer chooses an option. After discussing the choices available for resolving the problem, the patient/consumer should select one. Hopefully, one of the options is similar to the one the patient/customer indicated a preference for in the Customer Contact section of the discussion. If not, staff should stress what they *can* do, rather than what they *cannot,* and, if possible, provide an explanation of the benefits to the patient/customer of the alternatives. This takes staff work in advance to establish protocols for responding to the most common patient concerns. For example, when a patient/customer is not pleased with the offered appointment date and requests an earlier appointment with her physician, the Medical Receptionist may say:

"I understand you want an appointment with Dr. Smith. He is out of the office until next Tuesday. I can either schedule you for that day, or, if you need to be seen earlier, I can offer you an appointment this Friday with Dr. Jones."

Agree on the next step. The staff person describes in general terms what he or she will do next (who or which department will be contacted, what information will be sought, etc.), and tells the patient/customer when to expect a call back and from whom. The patient/customer should agree with the timeliness of the call back. This will also reduce the patient/customer's level of anxiety and reduce frequent calls to the staff person for status reports.

Staff should "under promise and over produce" whenever possible. For example, it is far better to tell the patient/customer to expect a call back by the end of the next day, and to then call the next morning, rather than to promise to call the next morning and not have the information until late the next afternoon.

Problem Solve and Respond

Once there is understanding about the nature of the patient/customer's concern and expectation for resolution, and the patient/customer's feelings about the problem have been acknowledged, the staff can begin the process of investigating and resolving the problem.

Consult with others. Sometimes the patient/customer's problem is beyond the staff person's scope of practice or area of expertise, or the predetermined solution space. In these situations, staff should know whom to contact for more information and assistance in resolving the problem.

Consider options, exceptions, and education. Staff trained and prepared to respond to patient/customer concerns should have a range of options they can offer the patient/customer, as well as some latitude for choosing the "right" thing to do. These may involve explaining a process or system to educate the patient/customers and increase their understanding, or describing what the staff person can do to resolve the problem. If staff are unable to offer the patient/customer the requested resolution, alternatives should be offered that are as similar to the request as possible.

Contact patient/customer with a status report. If the problem has not yet been resolved, it is important to contact the patient/customer as previously agreed so that the patient/customer does not become frustrated with the process.

Refer/Respond

Ideally, most problems can be handled by the staff person who hears them. When at all possible, this staff person should remain the key point person for the patient/consumer.

Respond to patient/customer with resolution. When the staff person resolves the problem, the patient/customer needs to be advised of the final decision. The resolution should be personalized to match the patient/customer's medical and physical needs, as well as his or her emotional needs. This will be discussed in more detail in Chapter 3.

Refer problem to another staff person to investigate/resolve. There will be occasions, however, when it is appropriate for the staff person to refer the problem to someone else in the office, facility, or organization to investigate, review, and/or resolve. Keep in mind that the *problem* should be passed along, not the *patient/customer*. Staff should take these steps when referring a problem:

- contact the appropriate staff person and relay all the pertinent information and facts about the problem;
- negotiate with that staff person to assume responsibility for investigating, reviewing, and/or resolving the problem, including who will notify the patient/customer with the final resolution;
- advise the patient/customer of the next step, including who the key contact staff person is and how to reach him/her;
- document in writing the pertinent facts and the plan for resolution, and send a copy to the key contact staff person.

Following these steps will ensure that patient/customers are not lost in the process, as well as give them a clear understanding and agreement as to who is responsible for doing what. If there is no agreement, staff should know as part of the agreed-upon protocols whom to contact for assistance.

Follow Up

After there is agreement on the resolution to the problem, the staff person needs to verify what the patient/customer has agreed to, that he is satisfied with the resolution, and that he understands what happens next.

Bring problem to closure. This last discussion confirms all agreements and brings closure to the problem-solving process. The discussion should:

- review the outcome—before concluding the discussion, repeat the resolution, and obtain agreement;
- negotiate any additional follow-up—confirm that the patient/customer understands the next steps, what the staff person's role or continued involvement will be, and the patient's role, even if it is only to wait for a return phone call;
- the staff person should give his or her name and phone number to the patient/customer in case there are any additional questions, or if problems occur with the resolution.

Thank the patient/customer. For most patient/customers, it is difficult to voice a complaint. Thanking them reassures them that sharing the complaint was the right thing to do, that there will be no repercussions for complaining, and again responds to the initial feelings behind the dissatisfaction.

Standards. If it is appropriate for the situation, share with the patient/customer the clinic's, hospital's, or organization's standards for responding to patient/customer concerns.

These may include the following goals:

- you strive to recognize the patient/customer as an individual;
- you strive to provide the patient/customer with an easy, obvious process for sharing concerns;
- you strive to provide the patient/customer with a key contact person;
- you strive for a fair resolution;
- you strive for a fast resolution;
- you strive to provide consistent, clear, and accurate information.

Follow-up letter. In some cases, especially if the problem or resolution was complicated, if the patient/customer sent a letter, or if the patient/customer was particularly upset, then a follow-up letter to the patient/customer should be considered. (In Chapter 5, correspondence with patients is described in more detail.) Such a letter would include:

- a one-sentence summary of the problem with enough specifics for the patient/customer to know it is a personalized letter
- an apology to the patient/customer for the feelings of dissatisfaction
- a reiteration of the staff's interest in the patient/customer's satisfaction with care or service

Document the concern. Depending on the protocols agreed to by administration, physicians, and staff, the complaint may be documented. This step can be as simple as a check mark or tick mark, or it can involve a written narrative as to the patient's perspective of the problem, the staff's findings, and the resolution using a form such as Figure 6-1 in Chapter 6.

The steps cited above are not necessary or mandatory for every complaint a staff person receives. Most complaints can be handled with one discussion or phone call in less than five or ten minutes. However, depending on the complexity and the patient/customer's level of anger or frustration, other problems may require all the steps.

Atonement

Another component of Service Recovery that is used in many service industries is "atonement," or the "value-added" piece. In other service industries, this may be a free dessert to make up for problems with a meal, a free upgrade in accommodations for a hotel reservation error, or a certificate for savings on the next purchase.

In health care, there may be times when it is appropriate to write off a charge, to waive a copayment, or to offer a free cup of coffee in the cafeteria. Sometimes the television or telephone service charges can be waived. As management and staff develop service recovery protocols for their departments and facilities, this topic will need to be addressed.

The Service Recovery process works for receptionists, physicians, nurses, ancillary staff, business office staff, and administrators in all types of healthcare organizations. It is easy to learn, and the basic steps can be customized to the specific problem and to the individual patient/customer's needs. It results in loyal patient/customers who feel the staff and organization care about them as individuals.

NOTES

1. "Zero Defections" is a copyright of Bain and Company.

Chapter 3

Service Recovery: Additional Considerations

Chapter 1 described what Service Recovery is and why it is important. Chapter 2 provided an outline to the basic steps in the Service Recovery process. These basic steps can be applied to the vast majority of patient complaint situations.

There are, however, some additional factors that need to be addressed for staff to successfully implement the service recovery protocols:

- the "culpability scale"
- the "emotional overlay"
- the complexity of the issues and the depth of review required
- the patient's expectation for resolution

In his work on Service Recovery, Ron Zemke, of Performance Research Associates, identified a number of components that must be taken into consideration during the Service Recovery process. He calls these the "culpability scale" and the "transactional overlay." Zemke reasons that although attention to the patient/customer's feelings needs to occur before attempting to solve the problem, the amount of staff effort required to resolve the problem may actually depend on these other considerations. In health care, the complexity of the issues, the scope of the review, and the patient's expectation for resolution are additional factors that need to be considered when responding to a patient/customer complaint.

▼ Culpability Scale

Zemke's "culpability scale" expands on TARP's work, and addresses the issue of "who caused the problem."[1]

- Some studies have shown that up to 30% of customer dissatisfaction is due to customer error (didn't read/follow directions, broke the product, etc). In these instances, the healthcare facility's or the organization's representative will express empathy and regret, but may not offer options for resolution that would be considered "heroic." For example, if the patient/customer went to another provider without an authorized referral, then the organization's representative may resist making an exception to cover that service. The physician may be reluctant to write a retroactive referral for a service he did not recommend.

- Some problems may be the result of acts of God/Nature. If adverse weather prevents a patient/customer from reaching an affiliated or designated facility in an emergency situation, the organization may or may not choose to waive deductibles associated with services received from an unaffiliated provider.

- A third party may be responsible for misinformation that led the patient/customer to behave in a particular way. Depending on the situation, the organization or office staff may be interested in resolving the problem to the patient/customer's satisfaction (even if it is contrary to policy), and then take up the issue with the agency that misled the patient/customer.

- The clinic, hospital, or healthcare organization itself (staff, systems, etc.) may have created the problem. In these situations, it is important for the organization's representative and staff to take heroic measures to resolve the problem to the patient/customer's satisfaction.

▼ Emotional Overlay

The second issue is the emotional overlay: How does the patient/customer feel about the problem? Zemke refers to three levels: neutral, annoyed, and victimized. It is helpful for staff to have tools to readily identify these three levels of emotional intensity, and to have guidelines for when to call for assistance when dealing with these dissatisfied patient/customers.

One tool developed by Zemke and his associate, Kristen Anderson, to help staff remember this concept is to designate a color to represent each of the three categories, and use that code to identify the traits of each.* The following are examples of this concept applied to the healthcare environment. (Note: Not all the traits in any one category may be applicable.)

Neutral/Blasé Blues

- The problem is simple.
- Patient has no preconceived expectation for resolution.

---

*Reprinted from *Delivering Knock Your Socks Off Service.* (AMACOM.) Used with permission of K. Anderson and R. Zemke. All rights reserved.

- Patient is interested in problem solving.
- Resolution is not particularly "time sensitive."
- The problem presents no "risk" to the organization.
- Staff are accustomed to hearing general comments or suggestions from this person.
- This is an "average" patient/customer; for instance, not related to someone such as the organization's CEO, president of major business, or to the leader of large union.

Annoyed/Ornery Orange

- Patient/customer is frustrated, annoyed, and wants action.
- Patient/customer is functional but needs anger diffusion before staff can begin to problem-solve.
- Problem is of moderate complexity; may involve multiple facilities or providers.
- A monetary resolution may be expected by the patient/customer.
- Specific intervention by staff is required.
- There is a moderate level of urgency in resolving the problem.
- This is an "average" patient/customer; for instance, not related to someone such as the organization's CEO, president of major business, or to the leader of large union.
- Administration is accustomed to hearing complaints from this person.

Victimized/Redhots

- Patient/customer exhibits extreme behavior, is highly emotional and possibly out of control.
- Patient/customer is unable to problem-solve.
- Patient/customer is usually dysfunctional (may have known personality disorder).
- Problem is of high complexity, or the issue or expectations for resolution are ambiguous.
- Resolution is time sensitive, high urgency, and may be needed the same day.
- Potential high risk for the organization, either litigation or bad press is possible.
- A regulatory agency may be involved, or the patient/customer is related to someone "important."
- Patient/customer is not someone staff recognize as a regular complainant.

The staff can identify the traits applicable to their patient/customers as they relate to these three categories. The next step is to identify which staff should resolve different kinds of complaints in each of the three levels. For example, if patient/customers have a complaint about the quality of their care, the facility staff may formalize their service recovery protocols so that:

- The physician's office handles a "Blasé Blue";

- An operations manager, clinical-care supervisor, or section chief might address an "Ornery Orange"; and

- An administrative-level patient representative would handle the "Redhots."

The organization might decide that all "Blasé Blues" will be handled by front-line staff; facility managers/chiefs will be called in to assist "Ornery Oranges"; and all "Redhots" will be referred to Administration. It is possible that a "Blasé Blue" will develop into an "Ornery Orange" if the problem is not responded to well by staff. It is also possible for a "Redhot" to de-escalate to a "Blasé Blue" if responded to quickly and in a caring manner.

Figure 3-1 shows one way staff can triage patient complaint situations.

Figure 3-1 Service Recovery Triage Table

	Red Hot	**Ornery Orange**	**Blasé Blue**
Clinical Quality of Care	1. Patient representative office	1. Facility, department, functional manager or chief 2. Patient representative office	1. Primary care/specialty physician's team 2. Facility, department, functional manager or chief 3. Patient representative office
Quality of Service: Access	1. Patient representative office	1. Primary care/ specialty physician's team 2. Facility/specialty manager or chief 3. Patient representative office	1. Primary care/ specialty physician's team 2. Facility/specialty manager or chief
Quality of Service: Information, Service Delivery, Customer Service	1. Patient representative office 2. Member services supervisor	1. Department head, primary care/specialty physician's team 2. Facility/specialty manager or chief 3. Patient representative office 4. Member services lead	1. Department head, primary care/specialty physician's team 2. Facility/specialty manager or chief 3. Patient representative office 4. Member services rep
Financial Membership	1. Member services supervisor	1. Member services lead	1. Member services rep
Policy Coverage	1. Member services supervisor	1. Member services lead	1. Member services rep

Assumptions:
1. Pass the complaint, not the customer.
2. Whenever possible, manage complaints at the original point of service.
3. These are guidelines; staff is expected to use judgment.

▼ Complexity of the Issues/Depth of the Review

The complexity of the patient's complaint (lack of parking vs. misdiagnosis and treatment) and the depth or scope of the review required to resolve the patient's complaint will also determine the review process. One way to decide who should handle which levels of complaint can be determined by the amount of time needed to investigate and resolve the complaint, as well as by who is involved in the process. The following are components for different levels of complaint complexity.

Level 1

- Patient/customer calls with complaint: **Blasé Blue.**
- Staff person follows Service Recovery protocols, offers options, and complaint is resolved during initial phone conversation.
- No further staff action is required.
- Staff person documents complaint per Service Recovery guidelines (tick mark may be all that is required at this level).

Level 2

- Patient/customer calls with complaint: **Blasé Blue.**
- Staff person explains the policy/system involved with the complaint.
- Staff person follows Service Recovery protocols, offers options for resolution.
- Staff person makes one or two telephone calls to assist in resolving complaint.
- Staff person documents complaint per Service Recovery guidelines (may involve combination of tick mark and narrative explanation of resolution).

Level 3

- Patient/customer calls or sends written complaint: **Ornery Orange.**
- Complaint may include quality of medical care issues.
- Minimal medical staff intervention required to resolve concerns.
- Requested resolution may involve waiver of copayment.
- Staff person documents complaint per Service Recovery guidelines (brief narrative re. nature of complaint, patient's expectation for resolution, actual resolution; may use a form such as Figure 6-1 found in Chapter 6).
- Copies of documented complaint are sent to involved staff, inviting them to share their perspective.

Level 4

- Patient/customer calls or sends written complaint: **Ornery Orange.**
- Medical records review may be required.

- Requested resolution may involve credit or write-off of internal charges of a pre-determined amount, such as under $250.
- Multiple facilities/divisions may be involved, which requires coordination of review and response by a designated case manager (Patient Representative).
- Multiple phone calls may be made to managers and medical staff.
- Reviewers include only facility/division managers and medical staff.
- Patient Representative may draft customized letter for facility manager's signature *or* send customized written response directly to the patient/customer.
- Patient Representative documents complaint per Service Recovery guidelines (more involved narrative re. nature of complaint, patient's expectation for resolution, staff findings from investigation, actual resolution; may use a form such as Figure 6-1 on page 73).

Level 5

- Patient/customer sends written complaint or calls and is asked to put complaint in writing: **Red Hot.**
- Complaint is appeal of resolution from levels 2 through 4.
- Medical records are reviewed.
- Requested resolution may involve credit or write-off of internal charges over $250 or request for coverage of services received from an unaffiliated provider.
- Quality-of-medical-care concerns are reviewed by a facility-based medical director (or chief of staff) or by a specialty section chief of staff.
- Multiple facilities/divisions may be involved, which requires coordination of review and response by a designated case manager (Patient Representative).
- Risk Management may be notified.
- Divisional administration may be involved in decision-making process.
- Patient Representative may draft customized letter for division administrator's signature *or* send customized written response directly to the patient/customer.
- Patient Representative documents complaint per Service Recovery guidelines (detailed narrative re. nature of complaint, patient's expectation for resolution, staff findings from investigation [may be excluded from quality of care review files], actual resolution; may use a form such as Figure 6-1 on page 73).

Level 6

- Complaint is received from a regulatory body such as State Insurance Commissioner's Office, State Department of Social/Health Services, Medical Disciplinary Board, or Health Care Financing Administration (HCFA), *or* from organization's executive office, *or* be a Level 5 complaint "gone bad": **Red Hot.**
- Risk Management may be involved in the review process.
- Quality-of-care concerns will generally be reviewed through Medical Director/Chief of Staff's office.

- Extensive review by organization's Contract Administration division may be involved.
- Multiple facilities or divisions within the organization may be involved.
- Complaint may involve request for coverage of services received from an unaffiliated provider or credit/write-off of internal charges.
- Divisional administration may be involved in decision-making process.
- Patient Representative may draft customized letter for the organization CEO's signature *or* send customized written response directly to the patient/customer.
- Patient Representative documents complaint per Service Recovery guidelines (detailed narrative re. nature of complaint, patient's expectation for resolution, staff findings from investigation (may be excluded from quality-of-care reviews), actual resolution; may use a form such as Figure 6-1 on page 73).

    Other complicating factors may include

- ethical dilemmas
- conflicting evidence
- complex medical issues
- unclear policies or protocols
- unclear lines of authority
- number of people involved (e.g., large family), or other participants (e.g., attorney, guardian ad litem).

In a large, multifacility organization, Level 1 and Level 2 (Blasé Blue) complaints can usually be handled by front-line staff and supervisors. Level 3 and Level 4 (Ornery Orange) complaints can be resolved by facility managers or by facility-based patient representatives who report to those managers. Level 5 and Level 6 (Red Hot) concerns are best handled by an administrative Patient Representative department at the division level.

Small group practices can learn to handle Levels 1, 2, 3, and 4 (Blasé Blue and Ornery Orange) within the office, and may want to consider contracting for professional assistance with Levels 5 and 6 (Red Hot).

▼ Patient Expectation for Resolution

The patient/customer's expectation for resolution also plays a role in how the review will be conducted. A patient who wants $1000 in medical bills paid will require a different kind of quality of care review than a patient who wants to share her story so the physician changes the way he does something. Some patients want their frustration with the telephone system documented; others want to participate on a telephone improvement task force. What the patient asks for is often a good indicator of how upset he really is about the problem.

Fortunately, the vast majority of patient/customer concerns will be resolved easily by following the basic Service Recovery steps. Staff will feel less vulnerable and more in control of the situation if they are trained to identify potential pitfalls in complaint management, and if they know when—and whom—to call for back-up and assistance when the problem is more than they are comfortable with or qualified to resolve.

NOTES

1. J.A. Goodman, The Nature of Customer Satisfaction (paper presented at the meeting of the National Quality Forum IV, 1988, revised 1993), 6.

Chapter 4

Review Process for Clinical Quality-of-Care Complaints

Patient satisfaction with the organization's response to clinical quality-of-medical-care complaints is critical to the effectiveness and success of a grievance process. Using patient satisfaction as a goal can, however, represent a paradigm shift from the traditional Risk Management approach. Risk Management's focus is on reducing loss claims and protecting the organization from the "enemy" (that is, the patient or the patient's attorney), in what often becomes a confrontational, adversarial process.

In 1999, HCFA adopted six new patients' rights, including a "Notice of Patients' Rights and Grievance Process," that apply to all hospitals participating in Medicare or Medicaid programs, including psychiatric, rehab, long-term, pediatric, and alcohol-drug facilities.

Although not delineating specific acceptable procedures, the "grievance process" Conditions of Participation (CoPs) does stipulate the following:

- A hospital must inform each patient (or his or her representative) of the patient's rights in advance of furnishing or discontinuing patient care, whenever possible.

- The hospital must have a process for the prompt resolution of a patient grievance and must inform each patient whom to contact to file a grievance.

- The hospital's governing body is responsible for reviewing and resolving grievances, unless it delegates the responsibility in writing to a "Grievance Committee."

- The grievance process also must allow for the timely referral of patient quality-of-care or premature-discharge concerns to the appropriate "Quality Control Peer Review Organization."
- Minimum elements of a hospital grievance process include:
  - A specified time frame for review of a grievance and providing a response; and
  - A grievance resolution that includes a written notice of the hospital's decision that includes the name of a contact person, steps taken to investigate the grievance, the result of the grievance process, and the date of completion.

With this increasing emphasis on patient rights, the relationship between the providers/organization and the patients has changed. The healthcare provider, and thus, Risk Management, must treat the patient as someone whose needs should be met if the customer is to remain loyal, and the organization is to remain financially viable.

Aside from being a regulatory requirement, a quality-of-care review process coordinated or managed by highly skilled Patient Representatives can be a powerful tool to reduce Risk Management claims. Studies indicate that how staff—including physicians—respond to a clinical error, or to the patient's perception that there has been an error, affects the probability that the patient will file a claim.

A study of the impact of malpractice litigation on the doctor-patient relationship was reported by a team under the auspices of the Center for the Study of Bioethics at the Medical College of Wisconsin. From their research, the authors conclude that the incidence of claims could be reduced if the healthcare providers had a process for reviewing patient concerns. The process needs to be informal and nonjudicial, and it needs to be implemented at the time the patient perceives there is a problem with medical care.[1] Such processes enhance communication between providers and patients at a time when historically they have become estranged. This improved communication allows the providers to respond to patients so they do not have to appeal through the judicial system to receive a response.

It is not surprising that these findings coincide with the findings of organizations using Service Recovery to respond to patient or customer complaints. Patients expect a clearly defined mechanism through which they can ask questions about every aspect of care and service, including their diagnosis or treatment, and to receive answers in a non-adversarial arena—and at no cost. Making this available can be crucial to healthcare providers to avoid professional liability claims that cost considerably more in administrative time and expense. A clearly defined process also reduces the emotional trauma to the involved providers. Over time, such a program can reduce the claims rate.

In Seattle, Washington, a large HMO's patient relations departments followed the quality-of-care review process described in this chapter. Over a 15-year period, only a handful of the Level 2 through Level 6 (Blasé Blue, Ornery Orange, and Red Hot) clinical quality-of-care complaints that were investigated and resolved by the regional departments went on to Risk Management appeals, regardless of whether the patient was granted the requested financial settlement. Although none of the cases included requests for "general compensation," many of the cases did include a request for a financial settlement, from the write-off of a copayment to payment for services received from providers not affiliated with the organization.

Based on the same principles, an urban Seattle hospital implemented an early warning system whereby staff called for immediate Patient Representative intervention when a patient or family members were unhappy with the patient's care, when there had been a problem with care, or an unexpected outcome, which a patient or family member might interpret as substandard care. Reported situations ranged from surgery on the wrong body part to patients falling out of bed. In a two-year period, not one of those incidents turned into a claim with Risk Management.

What does this type of review process mean to those involved?

For patients, it means receiving a timely hearing of concerns and a prompt response to questions and concerns. The patients do not incur any costs, such as attorney fees, unless they choose to pursue that course. The process is timely because it is not dragged out for years through the judicial system before reaching a resolution. In many instances, front-line staff assist physicians in identifying unhappy or confused patients, so that concerns can be addressed immediately.

Physicians will potentially spend less time worrying about malpractice suits, less time with attorneys, and less time in depositions. This allows physicians to spend more time with their patients. For Medical Staff Administration, the "informal" and "formal" grievance processes described below provide prompt patient feedback. The information gleaned from the review can identify "quality-of-interaction" problems that may be corrected. Physicians often learn the hard way that poor "bedside manner" is more apt to generate malpractice claims than clinical-care errors. Management will appreciate having a process that works well to show to regulatory and accreditation surveyors.

▼ Nursing and Ancillary Staff

Staff expect to hear complaints from patients, but dissatisfaction with the quality of care another person has provided is probably the complaint that leaves staff feeling the most uncomfortable. If Management approaches the subject matter-of-factly, and the fear of staff ostracism for documenting a complaint is reduced, quality-of-care issues can be investigated and resolved in a way that meets patients' expectations and the organization's needs for quality assurance activities.

For specific Service Recovery protocols, the scripted responses for different staff found in Appendices A through E suggest how to respond to the patient.

Internally, the review of the patient's quality-of-care complaint starts when the staff person who heard the initial complaint documents it. A generic Case Report Form, such as Figure 6-1 on page 73, can be used by any staff member for any type of complaint involving any person, program, or system within the organization. The form should be completed immediately, and copies distributed.

One copy should be sent directly to the clinical-care supervisor responsible for the staff person named in the complaint. Depending on the severity of the complaint, the supervisor may call the staff person on the telephone or ask to meet with her to discuss the situation and options for resolution. The supervisor follows up with the patient, unless the complaint is very serious, in which case a higher-level administrator should make the contact.

In most cases, this review and follow-up with the patient will be completed within 24 to 48 hours of the patient's first contacting someone about the problem. Even in more serious or complex cases, a supervisor or administrator should contact the patient within this timeframe. For these complaints, it may be appropriate to initiate a review similar to the "formal" grievance process described in the next section.

A second copy of the patient's complaint should be sent to the person or department responsible for maintaining the quality assurance (QA), complaint, or grievance database. A third copy is routed to the appropriate managers, directors, or administrators. At some level, someone in the organization should be looking for trends or system problems.

▼ Medical Staff

Organizations have different approaches to responding to patient complaints about the medical care provided by physicians. The following sections describe the procedures used successfully by one healthcare organization. It assumes that the organization has a strong Patient Representative program (see Appendix H).

When a patient first contacts the Patient Representative with a complaint about clinical care, the patient's expectation for resolution is critical in determining how to resolve the issues or the problem. Depending on the problem and the requested resolution, there are two ways to proceed: the "informal" Service Recovery process or the more formal Quality-of-Care Review (grievance process).

"Informal" Review Process For Level 1 through Level 4 Complaints—Blasé Blue and Ornery Orange

Chapter 2 discussed the Service Recovery process. Appendices A through E provide specific examples of handling quality-of-care complaints when an "informal" Service Recovery process is appropriate; that is, when the patient is annoyed, but not hostile. These cases should be documented by staff and monitored by the Patient Representative department.

If the patient wishes to register the complaint so it will be "documented," and accepts the options offered to him for resolution, such as changing physicians or scheduling a second opinion appointment, the normal Service Recovery procedures apply. The Patient Representative assists the patient to schedule any additional care and documents the patient's concerns, using a "Case Report Form" such as Figure 6-1 on page 73.

Depending on the organization's Service Recovery guidelines, it may be appropriate to waive the copayment for the "second opinion" or next appointment as a good-faith gesture to the patient. Under "Resolution," the Patient Representative should record that a copy of the complaint was sent to the providers involved, and that a copy was sent to the appropriate section or facility chief of staff/medical director (depending on the Medical Staff's administrative hierarchy within the clinic, hospital, or organization).

A standard cover memo can be attached to the copy of the complaint, such as the one on the following page (Figure 4-1, Memo to Individual Provider). It may be used for any complaint involving a provider—Level 1 through Level 4 (Blasé Blue or Ornery Orange), medical care, attitude, or service. It can also be used as an "FYI" to alert the physician that one of his patients has contacted the Patient Representative.

Figure 4-1 Memo to Individual Provider

MEMORANDUM

To: _____ (name of physician) _____

From: _____ (name of patient representative) _____

Date: _____

Re: Patient: _____

Pt. #: _____

THE ATTACHED IS FOR YOUR INFORMATION ONLY

The above patient has contacted the Patient Representative Department with the attached complaint. Although there will be no further review of this case by this department, information from this report may be included in the Medical Staff annual evaluation process.

If you wish to make comments to include in our documentation, please forward them directly to me at (address/mail stop).

Attachment(s)

cc: Section/Clinic Chief

CONFIDENTIAL INFORMATION
DO NOT FILE IN PATIENT'S CHART

When the complaint is resolved, the Patient Representative's closed-case file should include the following:

1. completed Report Form (Figure 6-1)—required for *all* Patient Representative cases
2. letter from patient (if complaint was written)
3. letter from Patient Representative (if letter was written in response, rather than contacting patient by telephone)
4. progress notes
5. applicable medical records
6. bills or other pertinent information

"Formal" Review Process For Level 5 and Level 6 Complaints— Red Hots

Risk Managers and Patient Representatives often develop strong working relationships. Sometimes patients file a complaint that could be handled by either department. The following are brief guidelines for the relationship between the Patient Representative and Risk Management.

I. Basis for direct referral of a patient complaint to Risk Management:

   A. Patient has stated he is dissatisfied with the care provided, directly or indirectly asserting "negligent care," and is seeking

   1. Compensation for the alleged pain and suffering related to the care
   2. AND payment of bills for care received at another facility
   3. OR arrangement for special additional treatment to resolve the problem at no charge
   4. OR patient is threatening to sue or states an attorney has been contacted.

   B. Patient has retained representation of an attorney to handle the claim and request for general compensation.

II. Basis for advising Risk Management for possible consultation and/or involvement in the handling of a patient complaint:

   A. Patient is requesting consideration for a significant amount of bills (i.e., over $5,000) in relation to quality-of-care issues.
   B. Patient is unhappy or dissatisfied with Plan physician's opinion and is pressing to seek a second opinion at a non-Plan facility with the Plan covering the associated costs.
   C. Concern exists regarding patient's level of dissatisfaction with medical care, the significance of the resultant damages claimed, and an indication by the patient that future legal action is under consideration.

Unless patient/customers are adamant that they want general compensation, most complaints about quality of care can be resolved successfully by an experienced Patient Representative. If patients request general compensation, they can be offered a quality-of-care review, with the understanding that they can appeal to Risk Management if they are dissatisfied.

Most patients choose the quality-of-care review because it takes less time and does not cost them any money for attorney fees, and because what patients most often really want is for someone to listen and to answer questions. If the patient is determined to seek damages, the case should be referred directly to Risk Management. A case can always be referred to Risk Management, but rarely can a Risk Management case be referred back to the Patient Representative.

Sometimes the patient requests a financial settlement as part of the requested resolution. The Patient Representative's review should only consider specific out-of-pocket expenses. Financial settlements handled by the Patient Representative may include reimbursement for expenses from another healthcare provider incurred as a result of the perceived quality-of-care problem, or a write-off of organization charges. The "informal" process can sometimes be used if the patient is asking for waiver of a co-pay or for payment for one office visit. But for anything over $100 or where there is concern that the patient will consider payment to be precedent-setting, the formalized review by a skilled Patient Representative is usually necessary. These would be Level 5 or Level 6 (Red Hots) complaints, as described in Chapter 3.

The first step is to ask patients to put their complaint in writing. This request often helps assure patients that their concerns will be taken seriously and reviewed. Writing the complaint down often helps patients clarify in their own minds what the issues are and what they want as a result of filing the complaint. If the patient is unable or incapable of putting the complaint in writing, the Patient Representative may need to provide assistance. The written statement should include:

- basic personal information, such as the patient's address, phone number, and patient number;
- the patient's expectation for resolution (do not be surprised when occasionally the patient wants the physician's license revoked!—after the patient's anger is defused, the Patient Representative can offer other options that are acceptable to all parties involved);
- the patient's description of what led to the patient's dissatisfaction with the care or services provided.

A standard form, such as Figure 4-2, Patient Complaint Form) will help the patient structure the complaint.

A cover letter should explain what is expected of the patient, including instructions on how to complete the Patient Complaint Form (Figure 4-2) and advice about what the patient can expect from the process (see Chapter 5). A copy of the Patient Bill of Rights, a brochure describing the organization's complaint-resolution process and a self-addressed, postage-paid envelope are helpful enclosures to include in this initial mailing to the patient.

Figure 4-2 Patient Complaint Form

PATIENT COMPLAINT FORM

Name: _____ Birth Date: _____

Address: _____ PT. #: _____

Phone: (H) _____ (W) _____ Insurance: _____

BRIEFLY, WHAT IS YOUR COMPLAINT ABOUT?_____
_____
_____

FACILITY   DEPARTMENT   PERSON(S) INVOLVED

_____   _____   _____

_____   _____   _____

HOW WOULD YOU LIKE IT RESOLVED?_____
_____
_____

EXPLANATION OF CONCERN: (Please use other side or additional sheets if necessary.)
_____
_____
_____
_____
_____
_____

(Name of clinic/hospital/organization) is authorized to investigate my concern. I understand that this may necessitate a review of my medical and financial records relating to my health care.

Signed: _____
(Patient or Parent/Legal Guardian)

Date: _____

In some instances, the patient has sought care from a provider not affiliated with the organization, who the patient feels gave better care and service, or the patient wants a financial settlement to pay the related bills. In these cases, a consent to release medical records should also be included with the Patient Complaint Form (Figure 4-2). This allows the patient's records from the other healthcare organization to be sent directly to the Patient Representative.

When the patient's written complaint, the patient's medical records, and records from the other organization have arrived, the Patient Representative then compiles a packet of information for each provider involved in the care of the patient for that particular condition.

These packets include:

I. Packet for providers involved in care of patient for this condition
   A. Figure 4-3: Cover memo with request for written response to Chief of Staff Office in five working days. Memo is cc:'d to Chief of Staff, physician's facility/section chief (for information), physician's facility manager (for information), and, if applicable, provider's preceptor (for information).
   B. Figure 4-2: Copy of patient's written complaint.
   C. Copy of patient's medical records that are relevant to the complaint, in chronological order.
   D. Copy of non-Plan medical records, if applicable.

II. Packet for Chief of Staff (or designated physician administrator)
   A. Figure 4-4: Cover memo with request for response to Patient Representative in eight working days. If financial settlement is requested, state the amount.
   B. Figure 4-2: Copy of patient's written complaint.
   C. Copy of patient's medical records that are relevant to the complaint, in chronological order.
   D. Copy of non-Plan medical records, if applicable.
   E. Anything else that may help Chief of Staff with review.

III. Packet for Physician's Facility/Section Chief; Physician's Facility Manager; Provider's Preceptor
   A. Figure 4-3: Copy of cover memo to physician.
   B. Figure 4-2: Copy of patient's written complaint.

All packets should be sealed in an envelope marked:
"CONFIDENTIAL—OPEN BY ADDRESSEE ONLY"

All copies of patient's written complaint and cover memos should be clearly marked:
"CONFIDENTIAL INFORMATION—DO NOT FILE IN PATIENT'S CHART"

The packet is sent to organization physicians cited in the complaint, as well as to other physicians within the organization who treated the patient for the same condition or illness.

Indicating in the cover memo (Figure 4-3) that the Chief of Staff is doing the review (rather than the Patient Representative) tends to ensure that responses will be sent within the prescribed timeframe.

Figure 4-3 Cover Memo to Providers Reviewing Patient Complaint

---

MEMORANDUM

To: _____ (name of physician) _____

From: _____ (name of patient representative) _____

Date: _____

Re: Patient: _____

Pt. #: _____

_____ , Chief of Staff/Medical Director (for Primary Care Services/Specialty Services/Hospital Services/Ambulatory Services, etc.) will be reviewing the attached concern. We would appreciate your review of this material since you were involved in the care of this patient.

1. Please comment regarding the diagnosis and treatment plan and any other information you feel will be helpful or pertinent to the case.

2. THIS IS CONFIDENTIAL INFORMATION. PLEASE DO NOT FILE IN PATIENT'S CHART. IF YOU WISH TO CONTACT THE PATIENT DIRECTLY CONCERNING THIS COMPLAINT, PLEASE CALL ME FIRST.

3. Please respond to the Chief of Staff by (give date for five working days after packet is being mailed). Return the attached packet to (name of someone who will collect them), Medical Staff Office, (address/mail stop).

Thank you for participating in the review. Your comments will help us respond to the patient.

Attachment(s)

cc: Chief of Staff
    (Facility Manager/Administrator) — FYI
    (Clinic/Section Chief) — FYI

CONFIDENTIAL INFORMATION
DO NOT FILE IN PATIENT'S CHART

Note: Depending on state law, language may be added to protect the documents from discovery under the protection of the Quality Assurance Program.

The cover memo clearly indicates that the complaint is not to be filed in the patient's medical record, helping to assure confidentiality in this grievance-resolution process. Physicians are also asked to not contact the patient directly to avoid a confrontational situation. The facility manager/administrator and the section/clinic chief receive a copy of the cover memo and a copy of the patient's written complaint. It is not necessary to send them copies of the records, unless the Chief of Staff wants them to participate in the review.

In addition to the packet of information and copies of the cover memos sent to the involved physicians, a cover memo (Figure 4-4) is also sent to the Chief of Staff.

When all the physicians have responded, the Chief of Staff (or designated physician administrator) reviews them within the next three working days. Then, the Chief of Staff meets with the Patient Representative to review the responses, discuss the case, including any extenuating circumstances, and agree on an equitable resolution. Within the next two working days, the Patient Representative drafts a letter, which the Chief of Staff reviews for technical medical accuracy. Sample language for these letters is found in Chapter 5. The final letter is mailed to the patient, with a copy to the Chief of Staff Office, and "blind copies" to the physicians involved in the review.

Proper documentation of cases is important to the credibility of the grievance process. Consistency and order in storing the complaints enhances the retrievability of information later, and in auditing the grievance process.

Because of their size, it is usually helpful for the Patient Representative to store these case records in some type of folder with pockets, and have all case contents filed in a consistent order for easy information retrieval.

Contents Of Level 5 And Level 6 Case Files*

I. Left Side

    A. Patient Representative's completed Report Form (Figure 6-1 on page 73)

    B. Patient's written complaint (Figure 4-2)

    C. Copy of final letter to patient

    D. Progress notes

    E. Correspondence with patient (chronological order)

    F. Memos (copies) to physicians, administrators, etc. (Figures 4-3 and 4-4)

II. Right Side

    A. Copies of all bills, with summary sheet and total

    B. Copy of patient's medical records applicable to complaint

    C. Non-Plan records, if applicable

    D. Other pertinent information (e.g., articles, copies of policies, etc.)

* Assumes case is filed in folder with pockets on each side; can also be filed in three-ring binder with tabs.

Figure 4-4 Cover Memo to Chief of Staff Reviewing Patient Complaint

MEMORANDUM

To: _____ (name of Chief of Staff) _____

From: _____ (name of patient representative) _____

Date: _____

Re: Patient: _____

      Pt. #: _____

This patient has contacted me with the attached concern. Please review the enclosed packet and the comments from the providers involved in the case, and report your findings to me by (give date for eight working days after packet being mailed).

The following providers were named in the complaint and have been asked to respond to you by (give date five working days from the date the packet was mailed):

1.

2.

3.

The following providers have also been asked to review the complaint and respond to you:

1.

2.

3.

THIS IS CONFIDENTIAL INFORMATION. PLEASE DO NOT FILE IN THE PATIENT'S CHART.

Thank you.

Attachment(s)

Figure 4-5 Chief of Staff Worksheet for Reviewing Patient Complaints

LEVEL 5 OR LEVEL 6 (RED HOT) **PATIENT REPRESENTATIVE CASE**

Patient: _____

Respondents: _____

_____

_____

If not all physicians have responded, please either call the respondent or review the case without their response by (give date the Chief is supposed to contact the Patient Representative with a final response):

___ No MD Deficiency (Please indicate type below):
___ Questionable quality of interaction
___ Insurance coverage issue
___ Patient poor historian
___ Other: _____

___ Possible MD Deficiency

___ MD Deficiency
Comments: _____

_____

_____

Deficiency Indicators: (Chief of Staff's initials)
* Technical Quality of Care   Reviewer
* Continuity of Care
* Chart Documentation

_____
(Date Patient Rep notified)

Figure 4-6 Procedure for Formal Medical Staff Review of Quality-of-Care Complaints

Procedure	Time Frame
1. Patient contacts Patient Representative and is mailed complaint form for signature, and medical records release form if non-Plan care was received.	Sent within one working day
2. a. If patient does not respond, a letter is sent, encouraging patient to follow up with concern.	Written within 15 working days
b. If non-Plan care is involved, and records have not arrived, a letter is sent advising the patient to follow up with the non-Plan provider.	Written within 15 days after Patient Representative receives signed complaint form from patient
c. Patient returns signed complaint form; acknowledgment letter is sent to patient.	Written within one working day
3. Packet of information is compiled containing applicable medical records, the patient's letter, and any other appropriate information.	Sent within 2 working days of receiving all necessary info
a. Follow-up letter is sent to patient advising that review has been initiated and will take up to three weeks to complete.	Written within 1 working day
b. Medical Staff providers involved in complaint are sent a packet by Patient Representative, and asked to review the contents and report their findings to the Chief of Staff.	Respond within 2 working days of receiving packet
c. The Chief of Staff is sent packet and asked to review the contents and responses, and report his findings to the Patient Representative.	Respond within 8 working days of receiving the packet
d. If non-Medical Staff providers (i.e., RNs, MAs, or other providers who do not report to the Medical Staff) are involved in the complaint, the Chief of Staff office will contact the appropriate supervisor and the provider directly for their comments.	
4. Patient Representative writes a draft letter advising the patient of the results of the review, and sends it to Chief of Staff for approval.	Written within 2 working days of receiving the Chief of Staff's response
5. Patient Representative sends letter to patient, advising of the results of the review.	Sent within 1 working day of receiving comments from Chief of Staff regarding draft

The Medical Staff Office keeps information on the complaint in the physicians' files for Peer Review purposes. The information would include:

A. Copy of the Patient Complaint Form (Figure 4-2)

B. Copy of the final letter from the Patient Representative

C. The Chief of Staff Worksheet Reviewing Patient Complaints (Figure 4-5), which is completed by the Chief of Staff when the case is resolved

To reduce storage space, the physicians' written responses may be destroyed, depending on Risk Management's assessment of individual state laws concerning discovery. Each organization will make its own decision about discovery. However, the decision to not implement this grievance process should not be made based on fear of discovery. If the grievance process is done well, discovery becomes a nonissue.

Most patient complaints that are reviewed using this formal grievance process can be resolved within four to six weeks of the patient's first contact with the Patient Representative. The length of time often depends on how quickly the Patient Representative receives the patient's written statement and the unaffiliated provider's medical records.

Patients surveyed after this type of review indicated a high level of satisfaction with the grievance process. They felt "heard" by the organization and were not interested in pursuing the complaint further. As would be expected, those who obtained their requested financial settlement were more satisfied with the process than those who did not.

However, patients indicated their questions had been answered, and they had a clearer understanding of their diagnosis and treatment. They also reported high satisfaction and very positive comments about the caring and professional manner of the Patient Representatives who handled their complaints, *regardless of the outcome.*

NOTES

1. R.S. Shapiro, et al. A Survey of Sued and Nonsued Physicians and Suing Patients. *Archives of Internal Medicine.* 149 (October, 1989): 2190–2196.

Chapter 5

Correspondence with Patients

Business writing is supposed to be straightforward, expository communication. Instead, it is often a jargon-laden jumble that even those with a masters degree struggle to understand. Sending a letter like this to an already upset patient will do nothing to improve the relationship.

Written communication to a patient during the complaint resolution process should be clear, concise, professional, and at no more than an eighth-grade reading level. It should also have a personal, caring, empathetic, and nonbureaucratic tone. Patients reading the letters must feel they were written by a real person, by someone who is genuinely interested in the patient's concerns and satisfaction with care and services.

▼ Initial Letters

Service Recovery protocols work well in the majority of situations. The problem is usually solved with only a phone call. Other patient concerns are more complex and require a greater depth of investigation and review than is offered by normal Service Recovery protocols. These Level 5 and Level 6 "Red Hot" cases (see Chapter 3) generally require written communication between the Patient Representative and the patient.

After the initial patient contact, the Patient Representative follows up with a written request for more information. That request must do a number of things. It must state:

- why the letter is being sent (in response to patient's call or letter)
- what is expected of the patient
- what the patient can expect from the review process

The letter must also convey genuine interest on the part of the Patient Representative in investigating the patient's concerns. This letter should be written as close to the fifth-grade level as possible so that the patient understands what is said. This means shorter, simpler sentences and no jargon, acronyms, or alphabet soup.

In addition to the letter, the mailing might include a copy of the "Patient Bill of Rights," a brochure that describes the organization's complaint-resolution process, a form that assists the patient in documenting the complaint (see Chapter 4, Figure 4-2), and a stamped return envelope. If medical records from an unaffiliated facility are involved, a medical records release form should also be included.

The following are sample letters that can be modified to fit the particular situation.

Letter to Patient—Complaint Form Only

Dear [patient name]:

Thank you for calling our office today about the care you received at Madrona Clinic. I am sorry you were upset after your appointment, and I would be happy to have the problem reviewed. Before I begin the review, I will need your complaint in writing.

Your statement should describe what happened and why you are dissatisfied. You may use the enclosed Patient Complaint Form for this. Also, please include a statement about what you would like to have happen as a result of this review, or how you would like the problem resolved.

As soon as I receive your completed form, I will begin the review. When the review is finished, I will contact you by letter. However, please feel free to call me if you have any questions or need more information about the review process.

Thank you for bringing this matter to our attention.

Sincerely,

Patient Representative

(*Note:* The apology in the second sentence responds only to the patient's feelings.)

Other Variations on the Initial Letter

(1) I am writing to follow up on your husband's [wife's] telephone call. He [she] told me you had some problems with your recent medical care at Madrona Clinic . . . . Please include a statement about what you would like to have happen as a result of this review, or how you would like the problem resolved.

If you would like me to work with your husband [wife] on this problem, please write a sentence that he [she] is authorized to act as your representative. This is necessary to protect your rights to confidentiality and privacy.

(2) I received your letter about the problems you had with your care at Madrona Clinic. I am sorry you were dissatisfied with the services there . . . .

Before I begin the review, I need you to complete the top portion of the enclosed Patient Complaint Form and to sign at the bottom. Your letter can serve as your written statement.

Also, please include a statement about what you would like to have happen as a result of this review, or how you would like the problem resolved.

Letter to Patient—Bills and Medical Records

Dear [patient name]:

Thank you for calling our office today about the care you received at Madrona Hospital. I am sorry you were upset after your appointment, and I would be happy to review the problem. Before I begin the review, I will need the following:

1. **A Written Statement** describing what happened, and why you are dissatisfied with the care you received at Madrona Hospital.
[**And/or**] why you obtained care at a facility not affiliated with [organization] and the specific kind of medical care you received there. Also, please include a statement about what you would like to have happen as a result of this review, or how you would like the problem resolved. Please use the enclosed Patient Complaint Form for this.
2. **Your Medical Record from the Provider Not Affiliated with [Organization]**. Please sign the enclosed Medical Release form(s) and send them directly to the other physicians [hospitals] who treated you. A copy of your records will then be mailed directly to me.
3. **Copies of Bills from the Other Providers.*** Because these reviews take time, you may want to go ahead and make payment arrangements with Community Memorial Hospital. Madrona Hospital will then reimburse you directly should a decision be made to pay those bills.

A return envelope is enclosed for your convenience. If at any time you have questions about the review process, please call me. Thank you for bringing this matter to our attention.

Sincerely,
Patient Representative

**Note:* This is applicable if the patient is requesting that the Patient Representative authorize payment for care received from another organization, or if the patient's allegations are substantiated by another organization's providers. If the patient is requesting a write-off of bills from the Patient Representative's organization, information about the amount should be available from Accounts Receivable.

▼ Follow-Up Letters

After the initial packet is mailed, it is important to continue corresponding with the patient, keeping him apprised of the status of the review. Frequently patients do not return the completed Patient Complaint form. If the patient does not respond after three weeks, send a follow-up letter. The example on page 51 indicates interest in assisting the patient, sets a deadline for the patient to respond, and notifies the patient that the case will be closed if there is no response. Also, if for some reason the patient did not receive the packet, the letter indicates the Patient Representative did follow up after the initial contact, and perhaps there was a problem with the mail.

If the patient does not respond, either by returning the completed form, or by calling and saying "I've been so busy with the holidays/a new baby/etc., and I'll return the form as soon as possible," then the Patient Representative can close the case. The form for documenting complaints should be completed (see Figure 6-1 on page 73). If a physician was involved in the complaint, a copy should be sent to him or her with a cover memo (see Figure 4-1 on page 33).

Follow-Up Letter—Patient Has Not Returned Patient Complaint Form

Dear [patient name]:

On [date], I sent you a Patient Complaint form because you asked for an administrative review of your complaint. To date, I have not received your completed form.

I am interested in reviewing your concerns, but have found that too long a delay can make the review more difficult. If you have not contacted me within a week, I will assume that you do not wish to file a formal complaint. I will then document the information you have already given me, and will follow our usual procedure for sharing the information with (administration/medical staff).

Thank you for contacting us about your concerns. It is important to me that you are satisfied with the care and service you receive from us.

Sincerely,
Patient Representative

▼ Progress Report Letters

If the patient does respond, the patient needs to be apprised of the review's status. The next three letters are samples of "progress report" correspondence.

Received Patient Complaint Form But Not Medical Records

Dear [patient name]:

I am writing to let you know that I received your completed Patient Complaint Form. Your records from [name of provider/hospital] have not yet arrived, and I cannot initiate the review without them. It would help me start the review if you called [name of provider/hospital] and ask that the records be sent to me.

If you have any questions or need assistance, please call me.

Sincerely,
Patient Representative

Received Information—Review Initiated

Dear [patient name]:

I am writing to let you know that I received your completed Patient Complaint Form [**and/or**] the medical records from (name of provider/hospital), and have started the review of your concerns.

I will contact you by letter as soon as a determination has been reached. The review process usually takes two to three weeks to complete.

In the meantime, please call me if you have any questions. Again, thank you for taking the time to share your concerns with me.

Sincerely,
Patient Representative

Review Initiated

Dear [patient name]:

I am writing to let you know that the review of your complaint is under way. Although reviews can sometimes be completed in a few days, they can also take several weeks. As soon as the review of your concerns is finished, I will notify you by mail.

In the meantime, I did want to assure you that I am handling the review on your behalf. I will be in touch with you as soon as possible.

If you have any questions, please do not hesitate to call me.

Sincerely,
Patient Representative

▼ Billed for Copy of Patient Records

Occasionally a provider or hospital sends a bill to the Patient Representative along with the copy of the patient's records. The memo on page 57 is usually successful in crediting the charges.

Patient Representative Billed for Other Hospital's Records

TO: [name of provider/hospital]
FROM: [name], Patient Representative, Madrona Hospital
RE: [patient's name]
           [patient's account number]
           Invoice #

Madrona Hospital is part of a managed healthcare system. Although there is an insurance function, we also provide medical care to our enrollees. This department is reviewing some concerns of [patient's name]. A copy of the records for care received at your facility is necessary for that review.

Since we provide copies of a patient's Madrona Hospital records at no charge to other healthcare providers as a professional courtesy, other providers usually send us copies at no charge to the patient or to us.

I would appreciate a reconsideration of your bill for the copy of (patient's name) records in view of Madrona Hospital's role as a healthcare provider.

Sincerely,
Patient Representative

▼ Hold or Suspend Billing

If the patient requests payment of bills for an unaffiliated provider's services, or a write-off of charges, it is helpful to request the account be "suspended" or placed on hold during the review process. This demonstrates a personal interest in the patient's problem. A letter to the billing office or to the Patient Representative at that organization is usually all that is necessary. A sample is shown on page 59.

Suspend Billing

TO: [facility/provider/accounts receivable]
FROM: [name], Patient Representative, Madrona Hospital
DATE:
RE: [patient name]
                [patient number for billing facility]

[Patient name] has forwarded the attached bill to the Patient Representative Department. This bill is being reviewed for possible payment/reimbursement/write-off. I would appreciate your placing a hold on further billing until the review is completed. [OR] I would appreciate your holding further billing until I complete the review.

I will notify you in writing when the review is completed and indicate whether you should expect payment from us. [OR] if the charges will be credited.

I appreciate your assistance in this matter. If you have any questions, please do not hesitate to contact me at [phone number].

Sincerely,
Patient Representative

▼ Decertification

When staff determine that a patient no longer requires the acute level of nursing care provided by a hospital, Medicare (and some other insurance carriers) will no longer pay for those services. In these situations, patients may be notified that they are being "decertified," and must make arrangements to either transfer to a nursing home or return to their own home. The alternative for the patients is to stay in the hospital and pay the bills themselves.

When patients are decertified, most hospitals have an internal appeal mechanism in place. Decertification is difficult to explain to elderly patients, their spouses, and family members, especially when it is clear to everyone that the patient is still ill.

If the internal review upholds the original decision to decertify, the letter sent to the patient/family needs to convey this decision in a way that is as sensitive and compassionate as possible and that recognizes the patient's medical status. It should not sound bureaucratic, authoritative, or impersonal. The language should be clear and concise, and inform the patient of the available options.

The following is a sample response to an appealed decertification.

Response to Decertification Appeal

Dear [patient name]:

On [date], [name] from the Utilization Management Department told you that your hospitalization would not be covered by Medicare/your insurance after [date]. You requested an appeal of that decision.

The Utilization Review Committee, which includes three physicians, has reviewed your case. The Committee determined that the hospital's acute care services are not medically necessary for you at this time. The original decision that you are no longer eligible for Medicare coverage of this hospitalization was upheld.

This does not mean the Committee believes you no longer need any care. Rather, it means that your needs can reasonably be met in a setting other than the hospital.

You do not have to leave the hospital. However, should you choose to remain in the hospital, you will be billed for the hospital care you receive after [date].

If you wish to appeal this further, please contact me within 30 days and I will explain the next step.

Sincerely,
Patient Representative

▼ Results of the Review

The letter advising the patient of the action taken on his complaint or the results of a formal review must be empathetic and caring, yet still professional. The patient must feel he has been "heard," and that the organization cares about him as an individual. There are ways of doing this while still being supportive of staff and not compromising the organization in a potential liability situation. There are two levels of response letters:

- Response to Level 1 and Level 2 (Blasé Blue) through Level 3 and Level 4 (Ornery Orange) complaints about some aspect of service
- Response to report the results of an investigation of Level 5 and Level 6 (Red Hot) complaints

Letters for Level 1 and Level 2 (Blasé Blue) through Level 3 and Level 4 (Ornery Orange) Complaints

The Level 1 through Level 4 complaint-resolution letter is usually one page and includes basic Service Recovery protocols. It should include the following components:

- a summary of the patient/customer's request, the actions taken, and the agreed upon resolution;
- an apology for the patient/customer's feelings of dissatisfaction or inconvenience;
- a report of any system changes that have occurred as a result of this complaint, and a reaffirmation of the practice, clinic, or organization's commitment to quality;
- an offer to assist in the future if needed.

In the letter, the sentence "let me assure you that what you described is not the level of care and service we try to provide our enrollees" does not admit guilt—it is not saying that what the patient said happened did, in fact, occur. Another way to say this is "I am sorry the service was not what you expected." This wording is semantics, but it is important for the patient's satisfaction with the Service Recovery or complaint-handling process. When the patient feels the staff understand her perspective, then she is more loyal to the practice, the facility, and the organization.

The following is a sample response to these Level 1 through Level 4 complaint letters.

**Response for Level 1 and Level 2 (Blasé Blue) through
Level 3 and Level 4 (Ornery Orange) Complaints**

Dear [patient name]:

Thank you for your letter concerning [nature of the complaint]. I am sorry you were dissatisfied/unhappy/upset/etc. with our services. Let me assure you that what you described is not the level of care and service we try to provide our enrollees.

I appreciate your taking the time to share your concerns with me. Comments such as yours allow us to review the services we provide and to make changes where necessary. I have taken the liberty of sharing your letter with [title of manager/administrator/etc.] who will follow up with the staff.

[*If possible, briefly tell what happened as a result of the complaint, such as:*] Your letter was referred to the Director of Nursing Services for follow up with the staff. What you described is not the level of service we want to provide our patients. . . .

[OR] We agree parking can be difficult around Madrona Hospital. As part of our capital development plan, we are considering different options for increasing the number of available spaces . . . .

[OR] We are currently studying the telephone system to determine if we need more lines or if the problem involves only a few departments and can be resolved with some additional staff at peak times.

I am sorry you were not satisfied with the service you received. If you should encounter problems in the future, please call the department manager right away. The managers are very committed to making sure you are satisfied with the care and services you receive at Madrona Hospital.

Thank you again for taking the time to share your concerns. If my department can be of assistance to you in the future, please do not hesitate to contact us.

Sincerely,
Patient Representative

Letters for Level 5 and Level 6 (Red Hot) Complaints

Introductory Paragraph

The letter reporting the results of a formal investigation of the patient's concerns can be more difficult to write. It, too, should be empathetic and caring. The first section should tell the patient what was considered in the review and what the decision is.

> Dear [patient name]:
>
> Thank you for your patience while we completed the review of your concern. You had expressed concern about the care/service you received at Madrona Clinic for your [medical condition].

[Note: If review took longer than anticipated, acknowledge:]

> Although these reviews are usually completed within two to three weeks, yours was more complex than most and took longer.
>
> Some of the physicians involved in the review were out of town for part of the review period. We felt it was more important to give your case a thorough review than to finish it quickly.

> The reviewers considered your written statement and medical records, and concluded that the care you received was timely and appropriate (or appropriate and within community standards of care). Based on this, the decision has been made to deny your request for [refund/reimbursement/ payment for time loss from work/etc.]. I would like to take this opportunity to discuss the reasons behind this decision.

Main Paragraphs

The body of the letter must provide a clear and concise explanation of the basis for that conclusion. The following discussion depends on a number of variables:

- Was the problem an insurance-coverage issue?
- Was the patient's letter relatively straightforward, involving a specific incident?
- Was the patient's letter a copious outlining of multiple problems encompassing numerous providers?

Most final response letters from the Patient Representative should be no more than two single-space typewritten pages. Any more than that may offer too much opportunity for the patient to come back and argue over insignificant details. This main section of the letter should be clear, concise, and use laymen's English, not technical medical jargon.

Response to Policy Concerns

If the complaint involves a policy, the final letter should indicate what the policy is, its purpose, and how it is implemented. The letter should then describe how the patient's situation falls under the policy, why it was handled in a specific manner, and what could have made the situation different.

An apology is appropriately placed in this section. The following are examples of how to apologize: "I am sorry . . .

- "you were upset about . . . ."
- "you did not know about this policy in advance."
- "the explanation in the Certificate of Coverage was not clear to you."

This conveys concern about the patient as an individual, and acknowledges *his* perception of reality as being valid. Apologizing does not connote guilt in the liability sense of the word. Again, a patient wants to feel heard. An apology rather than a brush-off can build incredible goodwill and can create, or save, a loyal patient/customer.

Quality of Care

Concerns about quality of care should include a narrative summary of the patient's care—from the provider's perspective (i.e., what were the clinical findings, diagnosis, and treatment plan). Was the patient told to call the physician if the treatment was unsuccessful, but did not? Statements that are nonjudgmental but are a factual summarization are appropriate here.

Your primary care physician advised you to try the medication for two weeks and to call him if there was no improvement. The records indicate that at your *[date]* visit with him there was no mention that *[condition]* was still causing you problems.

Again, apologies can be very effective in acknowledging the patient's wish to be heard.

> Your physician regrets that you felt he did not take your concerns seriously. He would be happy to see you again to discuss other treatment options. You may call his office at ＿＿ – ＿＿＿＿ to schedule an appointment.

Closing Paragraph

The conclusion to the letter should show sensitivity and caring on the part of the Patient Representative.

> I am sorry I have not been able to help you with your request for a write-off of the charges.
>
> I know this is not the answer you were hoping for.

There should be an opening for the patient to call back if he still has questions.

> Hopefully this letter answers your questions [OR] addresses your concerns. If not, or if you have any additional questions, please do not hesitate to contact me.

▼ Transfer of Case to Risk Management

If a letter is well written, very few patients pursue the complaint any further. Most will continue to receive their care at the facility, although some change to a different physician. These letters are successful even in cases where the patient has discussed the complaint with an attorney, but has not filed any papers with the court. Once legal proceedings are initiated, or if Risk Management is involved, the Patient Representative may be advised to refrain from further involvement with the patient.

There are occasions when the review indicates the hospital and physicians are in a potential liability situation and compensation may be appropriate. The Patient Representative should work with or transfer the case to Risk Management for resolution and negotiation of an appropriate settlement. The following is a sample letter for notifying the patient of the transfer.

Transfer of Case to Risk Management

Dear [patient name]:

Thank you for your patience while we reviewed your concern. In reviewing your written statement, I found that you requested general compensation [**OR**] compensation for "pain and suffering." Unfortunately, I am not authorized to review that type of request. I have referred your case to our Risk Management Department to arrange the review of your concerns. A member of that department will be contacting you shortly. If you wish to contact them directly, they can be reached at 555–1234.

I hope all is going well with you and regret I cannot be the one to assist you with resolving this issue. If I can be of assistance in the future, please do not hesitate to call me.

Sincerely,
Patient Representative

▼ Financial Settlements

There are occasions when the technical quality of the care was appropriate but the communication or service may not have been the best. There are also situations reviewed by the Patient Representative that have the potential for professional liability.

In many cases, the patient requests reimbursement for out-of-pocket expenses, but not compensatory damages. The skilled Patient Representative should have authority to settle these cases. In the hospital setting, many Patient Representatives have authorization to adjust bills to resolve patient complaints, as well as a budget for this purpose. This assures that the case is handled smoothly, and that patients are not so frustrated by the process that they hire an attorney—again, simply because they want to be heard by the organization.

A letter to fit these situations might look like the one shown on page 69.

Granting Financial Settlements

Dear [patient name]:

Thank you for your patience while we completed the review of your concern. The reviewers considered your written statement as well as the records of your care. They found that while the care you received was technically appropriate, the communication between you and the staff could have been clearer. Based on that, they recommended the outstanding charges be credited as a good-faith gesture.

I am pleased to have been able to assist you with this matter. A memo has been sent to Accounts Receivable requesting a credit of $[specific amount] be applied to your unpaid balance. The credit should appear on your next statement. If you have any questions, or if my department can be of assistance in the future, please do not hesitate to contact us.

Sincerely,
Patient Representative

Usually, patients are satisfied with this response and do not pursue th
ther. They have been heard, and the problem was resolved to their satisfact

All of these letters are designed to advise patients that the organizatic
in them as individuals and in taking corrective action. The letters follow th
Recovery protocols of acknowledging the patient, apologizing, giving inf
recommending a resolution (and the reasons for it). Although the letters f
basic format, each can be easily customized to the particular situation, w
patients' perception that their complaint is being taken seriously and that they are receiv
ing a personalized response.

Chapter 6

Documenting, Tracking, and Reporting Patient Complaints

Many hospitals and healthcare organizations have implemented Total Quality Management (TQM) or Continuous Quality Improvement (CQI) strategies to improve systems. Patient complaints can provide detailed information and data on how well systems are working *from the patient's perspective.* This information is useful and reliable only if the documentation is tracked consistently and accurately throughout the organization.

Before establishing a system for documenting, tracking, and reporting patient/customer complaint information, some questions need to be asked in order to understand why it is important and what is hoped to be gained.

First, who is the "customer" for the documented complaint? The *patient* is a customer because the documentation provides a written record of her concern. If a problem occurs later, staff can identify who assisted the patient previously, what the issues and expectations were, and the agreed-to resolution.

Department or facility managers are customers because the immediate feedback can be used to manage the department or facility and to share the information with staff.

Administration and the medical staff are customers for the overview or trend information that can be obtained from the complaint data and added to other sources of patient-satisfaction measurements. In some situations, Administration will request more detailed information about specific topics or areas of concern.

Risk Management and Quality Assurance are also customers because the information derived from complaints can predict future claim trends and identify system problems that need to be addressed.[1]

The second question is how and what information is documented and tracked or "coded" for reporting purposes. Think about the desired result, and let that guide the process. It is always easier to track more information and not use all of it all the time, than to decide later that the information was needed and have to go back to retrieve it manually.

Some Patient Representatives track complaints by the location they occurred; some track by the type of complaint. In fact, both pieces of information are important. Administration will usually ask for the total number of complaints by type (Service, Staff Attitude, Access), but this information is not helpful to the department managers. Not every department is responsible for, or needs to address, "parking" or "cold food" complaints. Department or unit managers will find regular reporting of trend information helpful about the type of complaints documented about their department.

Another issue that comes up is how to identify the complaint—is the subject of the complaint coded from the patient's perspective, or is it based on information obtained during the course of the review. For example, the patient may complain about quality of care, but the review indicates the problem was staff attitude, or the patient was abusive, or the patient wants the organization to pay for a noncovered service. To be consistent with other patient-satisfaction information sources, the subject of the complaints should be coded from the patients' perspectives, how *they* described the problem, not how staff described the problem (although this information should be included in the case documentation). For Quality Assurance purposes, it may be helpful to add a "root cause" category.[2]

▼ Documenting Complaints

To provide a systematic approach to recording patient concerns and their resolution, develop a documentation tool, or patient complaint Case Report form, that can be used throughout the organization. The ways in which the Case Report form is completed and the categorization of specific situations need to be consistent for all users of the Case Report form if the information is to be meaningful and useful. Accuracy is also critical if the information is intended for any type of trend analyses.

Whatever Case Report forms are used, they should be standardized throughout the healthcare organization, rather than having each department developing its own. It is also helpful to use standard-size 8 1/2" × 11" paper. This size, along with attachments, such as letters to or from the patient and internal memos, fits into most file cabinets for easy retrieval.

Templates of the patient complaint Case Report form can be entered into personal computers or into a networked or mainframe system. Printed forms with lists of the most frequent complaints heard by front-line staff are fast and easy for them to use (see Chapter 2, Figure 2-10). A number of commercial software programs are already available, and may meet the organization's needs.

Because of the amount of documentation that can be generated in a Service Recovery/complaint-resolution process, efforts are needed to streamline and simplify the paper process. Certain information will be needed for every documented complaint, and some information will be needed only occasionally. The following is a sample case report form used by Patient Representatives, and a brief description of the type of information that should be considered for collection via the case report form (see Figure 6-1, Patient Relations Case Report Form).

Figure 6-1 Patient Relations Case Report Form

CS Mgr.: _____ LEVEL: _____

Name: _____ Pt. #:_____ Open Date: _____

Caller: _____ Rel. _____ Plan/Cover/Grp: _____ Close Date: _____

Address: _____ # Wk Days: _____

Phone: _____ (Home) _____ (Work) Form/Records Rec'd: _____

SUBJECT:

_____ Qual. Care _____ Policy _____ Inquiry
(300–399)   (700–899)   (200–299)

_____ Cust/Serv. _____ Access _____ Abusive Pt.
(500–524)   (400–499)   (100–199)

_____ Serv. Del. _____ Info/$ _____ Compliment
(525–549)   (550–650)

Settlement Req.: _____No_____Yes

$ Req. _____ $ Grant _____

Internal Charges:
 2)___Writes-off   ___ Credit

External Bills:
 4)___Admin.   ___ Covered

LOCATION:

Facility	Department	Personnel	MD's #
1)_____	_____	_____	_____
2)_____	_____	_____	_____
3)_____	_____	_____	_____
4)_____	_____	_____	_____

CONTACT BY:
__Phone   __Letter
__Staff Ref.   __Walk-in
__Survey   __Regulatory
                    Agency

Patient's Complaint: _____

_____

Patient's Expectations for Resolution: _____

_____

Resolution: _____

Patient's Perspective: _____

_____

_____

_____

Staff Perspective: _____

_____

_____

_____

_____

Case Code # _____ _____ _____ _____ _____ _____

- *Case Manager* identifies the staff person documenting and resolving the patient concern.

- *Level* identifies the complexity of different types of complaints, as discussed in Chapter 3.

- *Patient Name* includes the first and last name of the patient experiencing the difficulty. Note: If the name does not readily identify whether the patient is male or female, write (M) or (F) next to the name. Anonymous should be used only on a limited basis since it precludes collecting other demographic information that is useful in analyzing complaint data. It can also be difficult to hold staff accountable for anonymous complaints.

- *Name of Caller* should be recorded if someone other than the patient is calling to report the complaint on the patient's behalf.

- *Patient Number* is the patient number, medical records number, or organization's identification number for the patient who is having the problem. If an alternative is available, do not use the patient's Social Security number.

- *Date of Birth* of the patient who is having the problem.

- *Mailing Address* of the Patient or of the Caller (if this person is authorized to advocate for the patient). The address is usually required only if additional information or other correspondence needs to be sent to the Patient.

- *Plan/Coverage/Employer Group* information to identify the type of insurance coverage the patient has, either employer group, individual/family, Medicare, Medicaid, or private pay.

- *Telephone Number* where the Patient or Caller (if properly authorized to act as the Patient's spokesperson) can be reached during the day for follow-up on the problem.

- *Open Date* is the date the patient first contacted the Patient Representative department. When the patient's written statement is requested, it may be helpful to also log the date that statement was received by the department, as the time standard for resolving complaints would begin then.

- *Close Date* is the date the patient is contacted by phone or the date a letter is mailed by the Patient Representative with the final resolution to the complaint.

- *Number of Working Days* is the number of actual working days it took to resolve a case. If the case initially opened on Monday the first, and closed on Tuesday the second, that is one working day. If the case opened on Monday the first, and closed the following Monday the eighth, that is considered five working days. If the case opened on Monday the first, and closed on Tuesday the ninth, but Monday the eighth was a legal holiday, that also counts as five working days. For complex situations, such as Level 5 and Level 6 cases, the counting starts from the day the patient's completed and signed complaint form is received by the Patient Representative.

- *Subject of the Complaint* is the topic of the patient's complaint. Staff sometimes have difficulty determining how to code a particular complaint. Appendix G provides a decision diagram for choosing the general subject category and a list of the specific complaints that are included in each category.

- *Facility* identifies the particular clinic, hospital, or other facility that is identified by the patient in the complaint. In single-facility organizations (as well as multifacility), it may be helpful to also differentiate between Operations and Administrative divisions.

- *Department* indicates which department within a facility the complaint involves. This is probably the most difficult to identify specifically. The complaint may be about "hospital nursing," but it is more helpful for the Director of Nursing Services to know that it is "ICU/CCU" rather than "Labor/Delivery."

- *Staff or Personnel* identifies the particular staff person or job title involved in the complaint so supervisory staff can follow up.

- *Financial Settlement Request* identifies whether or not the patient has requested some kind of financial settlement as a resolution, and, if so, the type of settlement requested. (*Note:* In order to expedite the Service Recovery process, the Patient Representative and some staff should be authorized to review requests and approve the payment of specific out-of-pocket expenses (see discussion about "solution spaces" in Chapter 2). Requests for general compensation or "pain and suffering" are usually referred to Risk Management for consideration.

- *Amount Requested* indicates the dollar amount of the financial settlement the patient is requesting.

- *Amount Granted* indicates the dollar amount of the financial settlement granted to the patient as a result of the review of the complaint.

- *Patient Access* identifies how the complaint was first reported to the Patient Representative, (i.e., did the patient call by phone, write, come to the patient representative in person, or did a third party intervene on the patient's behalf?).

- *Patient's Complaint* provides a brief description of the nature of the complaint (can use the narrative one-liner indicated by the "subcategory" code number in the Subject section (found in Appendix G).

- *Patient's Expectation for Resolution* identifies what the patient wants as a result of the Patient Representative's intervention. This is important to identify with the patient during the initial conversation. Some may want a full investigation of the situation; others will only want the complaint documented.

- *Resolution/Comments* identifies how the case was resolved, such as "referred to supervisor for follow-up", "appt. arranged for next day," or "cc: Dr. Smith for information and comment."

- *Patient's Perspective* provides more detailed information of the patient's concern. Will include the who/what/where/why and how of the complaint.

- *Staff Perspective/Follow-up* provides the "staff version" of what occurred. It can also document the steps taken by the Patient Representative to resolve the concern, including who was called and the essence of those conversations.

- *Code #* provides the case identification number for entering and tracking the complaint in a computerized database.

It will take time for staff to learn how to complete the Case Report form accurately and consistently. However, the results are well worth the effort. Good, usable information will be available for a variety of administrative needs.

Figure 6-2 is an example of a completed form.

Figure 6-2 Patient Relations Case Report Form—Completed

CS Mgr.: _LHO_   LEVEL: _4_
Name: _Janice Doe_   Pt. #: _555-12-1212_   Open Date: _04/04/04_
Caller: _James Doe_   Rel. _Husb._   Plan/Cover/Grp: _Ind._   Close Date: _04/07/04_
Address: _123 Main St., Madrona, WA 98000_   # Wk Days: _3_
Phone: _555-1212_   (Home) _555-2333_   (Work)   Form/Records Rec'd: _N/A_

SUBJECT:
3) _305_ Qual. Care _____ Policy _____ Inquiry
(300–399)   (700–899)   (200–299)
_____ Cust/ Serv. 1) _428_ Access _____ Abusive Pt.
(500–524) 4) _402_ (400–499)   (100–199)
2) _527_ Serv. Del. _____ Info/$ _____ Compliment
(525–549)   (550–650)

Settlement Req.: _____ No _X_ Yes
$ Req. 2) _5.00_ $ Grant 2) _5.00_
     4) _125.00_   4) _0.00_
Internal Charges:
2) _X_ Writes-off _____ Credit

External Bills:
4) _X_ Admin. _____ Covered

LOCATION:

Facility	Department	Personnel	MD's #
1) _Madrona Clinic_	_Fam. Prac._	_MR_	_J. Brown–0245_
2) _Madrona Clinic_	_Fam. Prac._	_MD_	_J. Brown–0245_
3) _Madrona Hsp._	_Lab_	_Tech_	
4) _Madrona Hsp._	_Radiology_	_Mammography_	

CONTACT BY:
_X_ Phone   ___Letter
___ Staff Ref.   ___Walk-in
___ Survey   ___Regulatory
                 Agency

Patient's Complaint: 1) _Phone busy._ 2) _Waiting room delay._ 3) _Provider's technical skill._
                4) _Wait for routine appt._

Patient's Expectations for Resolution: 1) _Report._ 2) _Waive co-pay._ 3) _Report._
                        4) _Payment of bill from Community Memorial._

Resolution: 1) & 3) _Complaints reported to management._ 2) _Co-pay waived._ 4) _Coverage for mammography_
            denied.

Patient's Perspective: _Husband called re patient's complaint. 1) Called FP's office 5X. Repeatedly busy. Finally reached receptionist who scheduled appt. with FP. 2) Waited 1-hour past appt. time to see MD, resulting in missed meeting at work. Pt. is same age as mother was when diagnosed with breast cancer. Asked for mammogram referral. 3) Went to lab and tech had to stick her several times to find vein; bad bruise. 4) Called for mammogram appt. and was told wait for routine referral was 3 weeks. Called Community Memorial and they could see her in 2 days, so she went there._

Staff Perspective: _1) MR said patient called Tuesday after a 3-day holiday, and phones were crazy. 2) MD had 3 patients who needed direct admittance to hospital that morning, affecting rest of the morning's schedule._
  3) Lab supervisor will review case and talk with tech.
  4) Patient's asymptomatic mammogram referral was routine. Patient went outside health plan on her own without calling to request earlier appt.

Case Code # _04-1023_   _04-1024_   _04-1025_   _04-1026_   _____   _____

▼ Tracking Complaint Activity

Resolving and documenting individual patient complaints is only part of the Patient Representative's job. Reporting useful, quality information to Management and Medical Staff Administration is another part. The patient-satisfaction data gleaned from anecdotal patient encounters with the organization is valuable when combined with other patient-satisfaction data for TQM/CQI, as well as for ongoing Quality Assurance activities, for reducing potential professional liability risks, and for improving overall service. The end result is increasing the level of patient satisfaction with the services and the care provided by the practice, facility, or organization.

The foundation for analyzing and reporting complaint data is a computerized system including hardware with enough memory to handle large jobs, and good database management software that allows for multiple cross-tabulations and statistical analysis to produce standard and ad hoc reports for the administrative customers: Administration, Medical Staff, and Managers.

Before choosing a system, identify the types of information needed. Be creative and try to anticipate what information will be needed by the three administrative customers in two to three years. This process will help avoid purchasing a system that is obsolete before it is fully implemented, or that is too limited in its capabilities.

Consultation with a programmer may be appropriate. Talk to other Patient Representatives to learn which systems they use, and what they like and do not like about their systems. Make site visits to see the systems if necessary. After identifying the information needs and how the reports should look, choose the appropriate software.

In deciding what data to track on the computer, identify the information needs of different levels of administration. Facility managers/department heads will want specific details immediately, and regular reports on trends, while the organization's administrators will want more of an overview, with additional details available if requested.

Which Information to Enter into the Database

The Case Report form is the basis for all complaint information, which is why accurate completion of the form is critical to the value of the data. The following is a summary of the sections of the Case Report form that can be tracked and how the information can be used.

- *Case manager.* Knowing who handled which case is important if the patient calls the staff or the Patient Representative department again, or if questions arise later about the particulars of the complaint.

It is also a mechanism for managing the department, assuring the case load is balanced between members of the department, determining if time standards are being met, and calculating the ratio of complaints resolved by Patient Representatives to complaints documented and resolved by other staff.

- *Level of complexity.* Patients want their complaints resolved quickly. The level of complexity can help determine if complaints are resolved in a timely manner. One to two working days is usually acceptable for Level 1 and Level 2 (Blasé Blue) through Level 3 and Level 4 (Ornery Orange); ten working days for Level 5 and Level 6 (Red Hot). This also indicates the volume of each Level of case complexity (see Chapter 3 for more details). The level designation can also be a tool for assessing the distribution of workload and for making staffing decisions.

- *Level 1 through Level 4* (Blasé Blue and Ornery Orange) complaints are usually fairly simple calls involving problems with a specific service or individual staff person, or requests for assistance or clarification. Basic Service Recovery protocols are easily applied in these situations, which will comprise the vast majority of the cases documented by the Patient Representatives at both the facility and administrative levels. These complaints should normally be resolved within one to two working days.

- *Level 5 through Level 6* (Red Hot) complaints require more extensive work-up and investigation. The administrative Patient Representative department should coordinate the investigation and function as the patient's liaison with the organization (see Chapter 4 for more information on how to conduct the investigation). Because timely response is critical for patient satisfaction with the complaint resolution process, every effort should be made to notify the patient of the results of the review and resolution within 10 working days.

- *Patient name* is important for investigating the complaint, retrieval of cases after they are filed, and for noting repeat callers.

- *Caller.* Sometimes the person calling to file a complaint is not the patient. It is helpful to track this information, especially if the person has a different last name than the patient (cross-referencing names in the database system should be considered). This is also a method of identifying if the patient has a hearing or language barrier and requires the services of an interpreter or a TTY.

  Depending on state law, if the caller is complaining on behalf of a child, and if that child/patient is 18 or older, the patient's authorization is needed to review the record, or to even discuss the patient's care with the caller. Need for the patient's authorization to discuss the complaint also holds true for complaints filed by spouses and by adult children of independent elderly patients. Depending on state law, the authorization may need to be renewed every ninety days.

  It is also useful to identify the relationship of the caller to the patient (e.g., self, husband, wife, daughter, son, relative, employer, other) and the sex of the caller. Studies using this system indicate that overall, women complain twice as often as men, but husbands complain on behalf of wives at the same ratio wives complain on behalf of husbands. Women were found to complain on behalf of children or elderly parents three times more often than men. This information seemed to be consistent with other studies that have found that women are higher utilizers of healthcare than men, and that women tend to make the decisions about when and where their families receive health care. The information can also be helpful in prioritizing service improvement projects.

- *Patient number.* This information is essential to differentiate between two patients with the same/similar names, and for following up on a complaint; i.e., ordering patient records, reviewing patient financial information, and so on.

- *Date of birth* is helpful in determining if the patient is a minor child or an adult child whose confidentiality and privacy must be respected, even with a parent. It can also be helpful in explaining or predicting some patient behavior.

- *Plan/coverage/group.* In situations involving medical insurance benefits, this information is critical for the review. In managed care systems, organization administrators find information about their different employer groups helpful when meeting with benefits managers and when renewing contracts. This information can usually be obtained from the organization's computer system.

- *Opening date* is important for a variety of reasons. When reporting complaint activity to Administration, the time period the incidents occurred may be critical for going back later to determine why there was a flurry of complaints about a particular situation. The date can also be used for filing purposes.

  The date the Patient Representative received the written complaint form is also logged for an accurate count of the working days needed to resolve the case.

- *Closing date* is necessary for determining the number of working days it took to resolve a case. Deciding to report complaints to administration based on the month a case closed makes sense since the vast majority of all cases are resolved within a day or two of the Patient Representative's receiving them. For the database, the *month* the case closed, and the *quarter* of the year, are helpful ways of reporting complaint totals.

- *Working days.* Monitoring the number of working days required to resolve a complaint is a useful Patient Representative department management tool. Tracking the number of working days to resolve cases can be used as a Quality Assurance standard for the Service Recovery process. It is a means of determining if system changes are needed in the complaint resolution process.

- *Subject.* The basic subject of the complaint is helpful for overview reporting purposes; raw tallies can be quickly compared to other time periods or other data. The *subcategory code number* (see Appendix G) can be used for more refined reporting of the complaint data. Sometimes it is difficult for staff to choose the correct subject and code. Appendix G also includes a decision diagram that can be used for staff training.

  Note: A patient may lodge more than one complaint at a given time. Each complaint should be logged, with the Category/Facility/Department/Personnel portions of the form being completed for each specific complaint.

The following are the basic definitions for each Subject:

- *Quality of Care.* The patient perceives the medical care received at the facility was inadequate, incorrect, or unacceptable in other ways. These can include both provider-specific concerns, as well as "system issues." Examples are patient perceptions of incorrect or delayed diagnoses or treatment, or improper procedures during treatment. In some cases, the patient has sought medical care from a provider not affiliated with the organization and is requesting coverage for that service.

- *Policy.* The patient disagrees with or requests an exception to an established organizational policy. These frequently include medical coverage benefit issues such as coverage for services not included in the contract or coverage for self-referred care with a provider unaffiliated with the organization. Other types of policies could include "no smoking" policies in the hospital, and Bill of Rights policies, such as access to medical records, and confidentiality/privacy.

- *Quality of Service* which includes:
  - *Access to Services.* The patient perceives that there are barriers to receiving the desired services. These can include:
    - Access to appointments
    - Telephone access
    - Access to the facility of choice
    - Access to the provider of choice
  - *Service Delivery.* The patient perceives a problem with the timeliness or the flexibility of services, or problems with comfort, privacy, or security while receiving service.
  - *Staff Attitude.* The patient perceives that providers or other staff are not as helpful, polite, or friendly as expected or desired (e.g., rude, abrupt, sarcastic, insensitive, condescending, and so on).
- *Financial and membership matters* involve issues related to enrollment in the managed care plan and billing service concerns.
- *Information.* The patient perceives incorrect or incomplete information was provided by staff about a policy or service.
- *Complaint handling.* The patient is dissatisfied with the way staff responded to a complaint.
- *Inquiries.* The patient does not have a defined "complaint" or difference of opinion with the organization, but is having trouble understanding some aspect of the services he or she is receiving from the facility.
- *Abusive patient behavior.* This documents staff concerns about inappropriate or abusive behavior on the part of the patient/family member. Chapter 8 describes these behaviors in more detail.

- *Facility.* This allows for separating out a particular clinic or hospital within a large organization, or perhaps between the operations and the administrative support divisions within one hospital or clinic.

- *Department.* As described earlier in this chapter, this is important when trying to differentiate between departments or staff.

- *Personnel.* Since there are often multiple physicians in a given specialty, and multiple receptionists, as well as other healthcare providers in a given facility, it is helpful to find a more specific method of tracking this. One method is to assign a numeric code to each physician. If the organization does not have a sophisticated security clearance system for its mainframe computer, or if the complaint data will be used on a stand-alone computer system, a numbering system that is different from any other used by the organization for the medical staff should be considered for security reasons. Otherwise, the physicians' names or some other physician identification system used by the organization can be considered.

If the complaint involves the medical assistant in Dr. Brown's office, the "Department" section would be marked as "MA" (Medical Assistant), and the "Personnel" section would be marked with Dr. Brown's code. This system is extremely helpful in identifying individuals as well as healthcare teams that are not communicating well or may need some additional attention. Assigning a code number to each physician allows for evaluation of the functioning of the healthcare team (MD/RN/Medical Assistant/Medical Receptionist), as well as individuals.

If there are repeated complaints about telephone access to the Medical Receptionist, the ability to identify which physician offices are involved tells the manager whether it is an isolated problem or endemic to the facility. Suppose there are repeated complaints about RN's—is it one RN in particular or are several generating complaints? Identifying the staff by a physician code number is helpful in making that determination.

An example of how this can be useful: After a major reorganization in healthcare team (MD/RN/MA/MR) staffing models, patient complaints increased dramatically. Registered nurses and medical assistants had different tasks than before, and some physician/nurse teams that had worked together for years were separated. Analysis of the patient complaints indicated that three healthcare teams seemed to be adjusting to the changes reasonably well. But the fourth team alone accounted for well over 50 percent of the complaints. Management provided additional resources for that group to help the staff adjust to the changes. After work with the staff on team building, stress management, and conflict resolution, the number of complaints dropped to a level consistent with the other three healthcare teams.

At another time, telephone access (busy signals when calling the physician's office) complaints were analyzed. Because the complaints were tracked by physician, it was determined that one receptionist had the fewest complaints—and the most complaints. Further analysis indicated that one of the physicians the receptionist worked for encouraged patients to call frequently; thus those lines were often busy. The receptionist's other physician had a different practice style, resulting in better telephone access to the office. If the complaints had been tracked only by receptionist, it would have appeared to be a performance problem, rather than a larger system issue.

Without the capability to differentiate staff in some manner, the appropriate interventions could not have been implemented in these situations.

- *Claim requested/granted/type of claim.* Most patient complaints will not involve requests for financial settlements. Requests for financial settlement that are reviewed by the Patient Representative usually fall into two main categories, each with two subcategories:
  - *Bills for services received from the organization's providers*
    - *Credit.* The patient questions the appropriateness of a billing or charge; i.e., feels the service should be covered per the insurance contract, is included in a previously paid fee, or a charge is too high.
    - *Write-off.* The patient recognizes a service is not covered or that it is billable, but he feels there are extenuating circumstances for having the charges dropped or reduced. Examples are situations where the patient was not advised in advance that there would be a charge, or was quoted an estimate significantly lower than the actual charges.

- *Bills for services received from providers not affiliated with the organization*
  - *Covered by the Contract.* The patient has received medical care or services from a provider not affiliated with the organization, and believes the service is covered under the insurance contract or referral agreement.
  - *Administrative Decision.* A patient requests the organization cover expenses incurred from a provider not affiliated with the organization, or some other "claim" (e.g., time loss from work) based on extenuating circumstances. This is usually associated with quality-of-medical-care concerns, where the patient required follow-up care elsewhere due to a perceived hospital or provider error.

    Cases with requests for a financial settlement should be tracked to determine the amount requested and the amount granted, as well as the commonalities. For example, if a specific policy is causing repeated dissatisfaction, perhaps something can be done to modify it. Or if a particular physician consistently does not satisfy the patient's expectation for health care, resulting in requests that charges be written off, the physician may need to improve his interpersonal skills.
- *Patient access.* It is helpful to know how patients initially contacted the Patient Representative, either by phone, coming directly to the department, or referral. The higher the percentage of people coming to the department, the more Patient Representative department staff will need to be consistently available in the office to provide immediate assistance. If most patients send letters, staffing can occasionally be sparser, allowing more people to attend meetings, conduct workshops, or participate in projects.
- *Code number.* This is the identifying number used for each complaint when inputting to the database.

▼ Reporting Complaint Activity

The amount of detail included in a report will depend on the direct accountability a manager or administrator has for the service area.

Facility and department managers should receive a copy of the Case Report form. Those people with direct responsibility for the facility or department will want timely information about the details of the particular incidents. With this information, they can follow up with staff or make necessary system changes, which will hopefully prevent similar situations in the future.

In addition to copies of the individual complaints, the facility manager will find a simple spreadsheet and/or graphs helpful to summarize the data for the relevant area of responsibility. Depending on the manager's information needs, and the sophistication of the computer system, reports can be prepared and distributed monthly, quarterly, or annually.

The complaint data can be tallied by subject, by loyalty factors, or by whichever sorting system works best for the organization. It may also be helpful to show the number of complaints per visit, or per enrollee, to reflect growth or expansion of services.

Although facility managers want information about their particular areas, administrators are more interested in "roll-up" information that includes multiple facilities or divisions. For easy use, the same report format should be used for all levels of the organization.

Spreadsheets, bar charts, tables, and pie charts are all tools that can be used for displaying complaint data. The data can be viewed as an isolated snapshot in time, in comparison to the previous month or quarter, in comparison to the same time period the previous year, or over an extended period. A narrative analytical summary and financial settlement spreadsheets can be added to make a complete report for Administration.

Sources of information about patient satisfaction include patient compliments and complaints, hospital discharge surveys, focus groups, patient suggestion boxes, market research surveys, and other point-of-service surveys. Analyzed together, the organization can identify areas of strength and areas needing attention to improve patient satisfaction with the care and services the organization provides.

NOTES

1. TARP, *Using Complaints for Quality Assurance Decisions*, (1997).
2. Ibid.

Chapter 7

Identification of Trends

Once the complaint information is documented and entered into the computer, it is possible to analyze the data to determine if there are any trends or information that will help Management and Medical Staff improve services. Some of the trend information will relate to individual providers or staff, and other trend information will involve systems.

▼ Trending Physician Complaints

Tracking and reporting complaints that involve specific physicians can be sensitive. Critical to the success of such activity, and the requisite follow-up, is the full support of Medical Staff administration for physician accountability. This is necessary for the technical quality of the care provided, but also for the quality of the interactions with patients, given the correlation between the patient/physician relationship *with* overall patient loyalty and satisfaction ratings.

As they work with the Patient Representative, physicians usually come to view the Patient Representative as a resource and staff advocate. As long as the Patient Representative solicits physicians' input and perspective, and works *with* them to resolve patient concerns, physicians will continue to support the program.

It is a given that every physician will have complaints—that is part of working with the public. It is when the number of complaints becomes noticeably higher than average, or when patterns can be identified, that corrective strategies should be considered.

Previous chapters discussed the process for documenting and resolving complaints, as well as the mechanisms for soliciting physician feedback and perspective. This chapter discusses the reporting of complaints involving individual physicians and using that information to develop interventions.

Assigning a number to each physician that could be used to identify members of his healthcare team (MD, RN, Medical Assistant, Medical Receptionist), and the use of that number as part of the data collection activity, was described in Chapter 6. Some physicians may find this tracking activity threatening or an invasion of their right to practice medicine as they deem appropriate. It is imperative that the documenting and reporting of complaints be done in a nonjudgmental manner, that it be presented as a tool to assist physicians improve how they are viewed by their patients and improve their organization's "report card" ratings.

There are a number of ways to log compliments and complaints involving physicians. The components included are:

■ the month/year the compliment or complaint was reported;

■ the subject of the complaint, such as "Quality of Care," "Attitude," or "Service;"

■ the patient's name;

■ a brief narrative of the complaint, or the one-line descriptors found in Appendix G. If the complaint was a Level 5 or Level 6 (see Chapter 3 and Chapter 4) quality-of-care complaint that was reviewed by the Chief of Staff, a reference to see that file may be more appropriate than a narrative description.

The following table (Figure 7-1, Physician Compliment/Complaint Profile) is an example of how the file of a physician's compliments and complaints might look:

Figure 7-1 Physician Compliment/Complaint Profile

James Smith		Family Practice	South Clinic
3/94		Compliment	
4/94		Compliment - 3	
6/94	Attitude	Pt. felt MD was rude and insensitive when she was seen for abdominal pain. MD responded that patient had history of drug-seeking behavior and he has recommended she receive intensive outpatient treatment for chemical dependency.	Jane Brown
7/94		Compliment	
7/94	Qual/Care	See Medical Director's formal complaint file - John Doe.	
8/94	Qual/Care	Pt. felt MD did not diagnose fracture which resulted in need for additional surgery and time loss from work. Pt. did not follow up with request for Level 6 review; concern referred to MD and chief for information and comment.	Hal Jones
10/94		Compliment	

The preceding sample does not reveal any obvious trends. In fact, based on the number of compliments he received, Dr. Smith appears to be a well-liked physician. However, if the Medical Director's formal complaint file involves an orthopedic case, the Medical Director may want to look more closely at Dr. Smith's technical skills in this area and recommend a continuing education program dealing with that topic. Or it may be that Dr. Smith needs to improve how he conveys information to patients about fractures.

The Patient Representative is in a critical position to identify possible problems for the Chief of Staff. Early identification and follow-up will save the physician, as well as the facility or organization, time and money by averting potential liability situations. The process will also assist the physician in providing quality care and service. The brief narratives included in the physician's file can provide a warning that more investigation is necessary. The actual Case Report (discussed in Chapter 6) should be pulled for a more detailed description of the patient's perspective. If a trend is identified, the Chief of Staff should be given a copy of the physician's file as well as copies of the Case Report form. The Patient Representative should tell the Chief of Staff what trend has been identified.

Sometimes physicians will be concerned when they see an increase in their patient complaint activity, and they will seek assistance from the Patient Representative. At other times, physicians may realize their privileging is up for review and they will want to know what the Patient Representative will be contributing to that process.

The following are some actual examples of patient complaints about physicians, the patterns that were identified, and the corrective strategies that were successful in significantly decreasing the number of complaints the physicians received. The brief narratives included in the physicians' files do not provide the whole story, but they are an indication of problems. Reviewing the patient complaint case report form provided the additional information necessary to pinpoint the actual trends.

Example 1

1. Mother felt MD's attitude was that they were wasting his time.
2. Mother reported MD treats her like a "nonperson," never calls her by name, and does not answer questions.
3. Mother brought son in for evaluation—felt MD barely looked at him, and then told mother that her child should "be institutionalized."
4. Mother felt MD would not listen to anything she tried to tell him about child's previous history and only wanted to focus on the results of one test.

Review of these complaints revealed the physician had spent 30 to 45 minutes with each patient/parent, but for some reason the parents did not feel they had received what they needed. Further review of the individual Case Report forms determined that the parents all were single mothers of sons with newly diagnosed, incurable problems. The mothers were probably suffering from "overload"—trying to work, take care of the children, and now learning that her child had a problem that would require continual monitoring and special attention.

The physician probably could have spent an hour with each of these mothers, with no difference in the mothers' perspectives of the level of service they received. The physician, once he was aware of this "profile," was more sensitive to the mothers, and during the appointment, he provided them with written information they could take home and study later. After he made this change, there were no more of these complaints for that physician.

As a side note, prior to this review and analysis, the physician thought the Patient Representative was more of a nuisance than a help. After the patient profile was developed and the corrective strategies were successfully implemented, the physician recognized the value of the service and began calling the Patient Representative for assistance when dealing with difficult patients.

Example 2

1. Pt felt MD criticized her for non traditional occupation.
2. Pt felt MD was rude when she came in, and he lectured her about smoking.
3. Pt felt MD was rude, abrupt, and condescending when she saw him for problem.
4. Pt felt MD kept interrupting her explanation of the problem by making counteracting statements.
5. Pt indicated it was not what MD said but his tone of voice that made her feel foolish and that she was wasting his time.

Although this physician's technical skills were excellent, it was clear that his interpersonal and communication skills needed improvement. Reviewing the patient complaint Case Report forms revealed a patient profile that was helpful for the physician. The patients who complained tended to be women between the ages of 30 and 50 with low self-esteem, and often a history of depression. The symptoms they described could not be clinically substantiated or diagnosed, and were usually physical reactions to stress.

The physician was given some specific behavioral strategies to try with his patients:

- Before opening the exam room door, he was to take a deep breath and put aside any other concerns.
- When he went into the room, he introduced himself, sat down, and asked the patient to tell him about the problem.
- The patient was allowed to tell the history without interruption.
- The physician then made a statement that would validate the patient's feelings or perspective, a sentence or two that would tell the patient that the physician accepted her description of the symptoms or medical problem. It could be something very simple, such as "It sounds like you've had a difficult time with this condition."

That validation was very important to these patients and often made the difference in the patient's perception of the physician's attitude toward them. The physician would then proceed to examine the patient and order tests if appropriate. At that point, the physician reassured the patient that the problem was not something serious, such as cancer, and that from a clinical perspective he could not find a cause for the symptoms. Because the physician had validated the patient in the beginning of the process, the lack of a clinical diagnosis was easier for the patient to accept, and not be left with the feeling that the physician thought it was all "in her head."

Example 3

1. Pt was concerned she had to "get angry" before MD would recommend she see a specialist.
2. Pt reported MD was disinterested in her concerns and gave a half-hearted examination.
3. Pt felt MD brushed her husband off and did not do a thorough exam.
4. Mother felt MD was abrupt and uncaring, and let her suggest treatment when she brought child in.

The patients who filed these complaints felt they were quality-of-care issues; however, review of the medical records indicated that the care was technically appropriate. This physician needed assistance with his interpersonal skills. The strategy used in this situation was to team him with a physician noted for good communication skills and excellent rapport with patients. This role-modeling technique was effective. The number of complaints dropped dramatically, and the physician began receiving compliments for his care and concern.

Example 4

1. Pt was upset MD would not give her medication she requested for condition so she went somewhere else for it.
2. Pt requested suppositories but MD insisted on oral medication, which did not work.
3. Pt requested prescription for nicotine gum, but MD would not give it without enrollment in a smoking-cessation program.
4. Pt felt MD did not warn him of possible side effects of suddenly ceasing to take medications for chronic condition.

The physician was very concerned about these complaints and requested an analysis of the concerns. What was interesting about these complaints was that they all occurred in the same month—the month he had planned to take vacation but his request had been canceled by his chief of staff. The conclusion was that the chief of staff should not cancel the physician's vacation plans in the future unless an emergency arose. Here again, the strategy seemed to work because the number of complaints declined and stayed low in subsequent years.

Occasionally a physician will be concerned about the number of complaints lodged against him and will want to review them. The physician's conclusion may be that the complaints are all "system" problems that he has no control over. A subtle reminder that other physicians are working within the same arrangement or structure and are not receiving complaints may be appropriate. The physician will need to make a decision whether to assume responsibility for the problems or to leave the organization.

Physicians who are not familiar with such a program may be reluctant to participate at first. But recommendations from physicians who have been involved in the program, as well as active encouragement from the Medical Director/Chief of Staff and Risk Manager, can make a difference. Including physicians in the process is critical to successful compliance with the regulatory standards concerning quality-of-care complaints, the emphasis on system improvements, and satisfaction ratings from patients. An organization may want to link participation with the complaint-management/Service Recovery program to the medical staff's credentialing and privileging process.

The following is a sample letter to physicians that encourages participation. It advises the physician of the existence of the Service Recovery program, and conveys the Medical Staff administration's support for the process.

Letter to Physicians

Dear Dr. [physician's name]:

We are pleased you will be working with Madrona Health Plan in providing quality health care to our patients. We invite and encourage you to participate in the variety of programs, special projects, and studies that are conducted at Madrona.

One of the programs in which all Madrona Health Plan providers participate is the Patient Representative complaint-resolution process. In a nonadversarial, objective manner, patients are given the opportunity to express their specific concerns about the services they received, have those concerns reviewed, and receive a response to their questions. This process is part of our compliance with accreditation standards, and it is an integral component of our emphasis on continuous quality improvement and patient satisfaction.

The Medical Staff at Madrona Health Plan actively participates in reviews of patient concerns regarding medical care. The Patient Representative staff organizes the information needed to review the concern. Attached is a step-by-step guide to the procedure we follow. Should a patient contact the Patient Representative to express concern about the care she or he received from you, you would be contacted to obtain your perspective.

We look forward to an association that will be of mutual benefit to yourself and Madrona Health Plan. Should you have any questions about our Patient Representative program, please feel free to call us.

Sincerely,
Medical Director
Patient Representative

Enclosed with the letter should be a copy of the procedure followed for investigating and responding to patient complaints, and Service Recovery training information for office staff, as well as any brochures the organization has on patient rights and the Patient Representative program.

▼ Trending Nonphysician Complaints

Analyzing compliment and complaint data should not be limited to physicians. It can also be used to evaluate the level of services provided by various departments. This information provides opportunities for review of the process patients follow when receiving services from particular programs. For example, numerous complaints may involve a particular procedure or service provided by the Radiology department, but the staff rotate within the department, so no one person always does the procedure. The procedure or service can be reviewed to determine why the complaints are focused on that particular service:

- Is there a difference in the check-in process?
- Is timeliness of the service a problem from the patient's perspective?
- Does the service, by its nature, heighten the patient's anxiety level?

Reviewing the complaints with the department manager and staff can help identify the root causes of the problem. A focused improvement plan can be developed and implemented, using a team approach to resolve the problem. Further monitoring of complaint activity, along with random satisfaction surveys, can determine if the implemented strategies are successful, or if other interventions need to be considered.

Sometimes organizations reorganize front-line staff and change the procedures for dealing with patients. Complaint activity can be monitored to determine if the transition is progressing smoothly, or if special interventions are needed. The complaints can reveal if most staff are adjusting to the changes but other groups or individuals are not. Staff members experiencing difficulty can receive special assistance with team-building and problem-solving skills.

Most system improvement philosophies shy away from pointing fingers at individuals, focusing instead on systems. This works well where the process is a repetition of the same steps over and over, such as in manufacturing. In service industries, each interaction between a customer and a staff person is a unique, independent encounter. No one expects every staff person to have an excellent interaction with every patient every time. There are some individuals, however, who seem to generate more than the average number of patient complaints about service or attitude. The compliment and complaint information can be helpful for the supervisor working with these employees. Individuals who receive a significantly higher number of complaints than their peers will need counseling, coaching, and other performance management assistance. Those who receive numerous compliments should be commended in staff-recognition activities.

Chapter 8

Dealing with the Difficult Patient

Encountering difficult or challenging customers is part of any job that involves inter-action with the public. For instance, a man discusses with a discharge planner the op-tions available to his 85-year old mother who has just completed her first round of chemotherapy. The discharge planner rattles off a list of possibilities, punctuating each with "Medicare won't cover . . . ," or Medicare will cover . . . ," and sometimes "Of course, she's terminal so . . ." Finally, the man loses his temper and yells at the discharge planner, including calling her stupid and incompetent. She notes in the chart, "Patient's son is hostile; may have anger management problem."

In this incident, the patient and family's understanding is that the patient is to have rehab and rest up for the next round of chemo. The discharge planner has twice the case-load any person should be expected to handle, and rehab beds are in short supply. She has seen so many cases like this that she knows the woman will not have another course of treatment. She focuses on what Medicare will cover because most of her patients have limited resources.

Staff face emotionally charged situations such as this on a daily basis. The patient and family have one set of perceptions and expectations while staff have another. The ex-tra minutes to discuss and understand those differences are not there.

Because of the complexity of the issues involved in many of these situations, the ques-tions that have to be asked are when is it allowable for patients (or family members) to raise their voice in frustration and when does it cross the line to staff abuse? When is a threat a throw-away comment, and when should it be taken seriously? When are chart notes an appropriate warning to other staff, and when are they a counterproductive way for staff to vent their own frustrations? When does the organization ignore certain behaviors, when does it try to change those behaviors, and when does it have a zero tolerance?

Before discussing ways to respond to difficult patients, we need to clarify whom we are talking about. The vast majority of patients and their families are reasonably pleasant and never create a problem for the staff. There are other patients who require more patience to work with, the patients who are challenging. And, there is the growing group of patients who are abusive to staff.

In this chapter, we will look at

- the annoying patient
- the challenging patient
- the isolated incident
- the abusive patient
- the system abuser
- the lawbreaker
- the people abuser

▼ The Annoying Patient

Sometimes staff label patients as "difficult" because they ask for something out of the ordinary, such as a scheduling, a service or a policy exception, or because the patients are frustrating to work with. Sometimes these patients are not really difficult per se; they are simply exhibiting behavior that is normal, albeit somewhat annoying.

What is annoying behavior for one staff person, however, may not bother another. One suggestion is to have staff think about which patient behaviors set their teeth on edge. Simply knowing what those are often de-escalates staffs' spontaneous emotional reaction. For example, some staff hate dealing with those who have a whining edge to their voice, while other staff have little patience with those who can't quite get around to saying what their problem is. Once these behavior types are identified, staff can discuss ways to work with them.

▼ The Challenging Patient

There is a group of patients who take a lot of staff time and, because of that, can be frustrating to work with. They are usually not "abusive" to staff; in fact, some of them can be quite pleasant. But because of the resources they consume, both staff time and services, finding ways to work with them effectively can make life much easier for staff and reduce their stress levels, as well as improve patient satisfaction.

Historians

These patients always start at the beginning—usually 10 to 30 years ago—and give the staff person a litany of their grievances over the years. It does not matter if the staff person has heard the story before, or if the concerns have been investigated in the past. The patient still insists on telling the entire story, from the beginning.

A strategy for handling these situations is to listen attentively for a few minutes, and then to break in with: "I know you were unhappy with these situations, and we have talked about them before, so what can I do to help you today?"

The staff person may need to repeatedly focus the patient back to *today's* issue, until finally the patient identifies that problem and the staff person can respond. This technique can reduce these encounters to 10 to 15 minutes, which may still seem like a long time. However, when the discussion is over, the patient leaves with the feeling of being heard, and the staff person feels she has maintained some control of the conversation.

Socially Isolated Patients

Many elderly people live alone and have limited social outlets. Calling their physician's office to talk to the nurse and coming in for appointments may be meeting a social interaction need more than a medical need. Because the patient calls frequently—and often likes to talk a long time—a potentially serious medical problem may be overlooked. Patients who fall into this category seem to benefit from regularly scheduled times for the nurse to call. Another strategy is to have volunteers call or visit these patients on a regular basis to help respond to the patient's social needs.

A social services assessment in the patient's home may provide useful information for the physician's office. Is it safe for the patient to continue living alone? Are there other family members available to help, but who may not be aware of the extent of the problem? In a managed care system, some resources to assist with these patients may be available that might not ordinarily be accessible to an individual physician.

Head Injury Patients

Because their short-term memory may be affected, these patients are difficult because they may not remember discussions and agreements after they are made. They call the office with the same questions, the same concerns, the same issues on a daily or weekly basis. Staff need to remember that this behavior is not the patient's fault, and that the memory problem is very frustrating for the patient as well. Sometimes the patient's support system (friends and relatives) view the physician's office or the system as the enemy because they perceive the staff is not responding to, or taking care of, the patient.

One strategy is for staff to cultivate a relationship with the patient's key support person as an ally in meeting the patient's needs. This family member, friend, or volunteer can attend appointments with the patient, write a summary of the discussion, treatment plan, and other agreements, and then regularly contact the patient to make sure he or she is following up as agreed. If the staff determine that the patient is not remembering the discussions or agreements, the support person can be contacted to assist the patient.

The Overly-Involved Family

Sometimes a hospital patient and multiple family members will create chaos on the unit by asking staff the same questions, and complaining to everyone who will listen.

Often it is those who come the farthest who are the most demanding; they aren't taking care of Mom, but have high expectations of the staff. A meeting with the unit manager, the Patient Representative, a social worker, all the family members, and the patient is a way to discuss concerns, explain policies, and set limits. Requiring the family to designate one person as the spokesperson for everyone, and designating the Patient Representative as the contact or liaison person can make the situation more manageable by settling the family down and allowing the staff to provide care and service to all the patients on the unit. In some situations, it is helpful for the Patient Representative and the family spokesperson to have a specific time to meet each day to discuss concerns or issues that arise. The Patient Representative then acts as the family's intermediary with the hospital staff.

The Noncompliant Patient

The physician may have occasions where the need for additional tests or treatment has been identified, but the patient is not following up, for whatever reason. The physician is concerned because the patient's health and well-being may be adversely affected by not following the recommendations. In these situations, the physician may want to send the patient a letter, either "certified" or "return receipt requested" to ensure the patient received it. Such as letter should include the following:

- a statement describing the patient's current condition
- an outline of the recommended treatment
- the risks and benefits of that treatment
- the risks of not receiving the treatment
- a statement of the physician's personal concern for the patient's health/well-being
- a statement that the physician cannot be held responsible if the patient does not follow up
- the phone number to call to schedule an appointment, the tests, or to discuss the situation with the physician

A copy of the letter should be added to the patient's chart, and a blind copy sent to the Patient Representative and/or Risk Manager.

Although these are not all the "challenging" types of patients, they include some of the most frequently encountered patient behaviors that staff find difficult to work with. Medical care and services need to be "patient focused." However, there are occasions when limits and guidelines need to be established if the physicians and staff are to meet the needs of the entire patient population they serve. Understanding the patient's perspective and motivation should help staff be more responsive to meeting their needs.

▼ The Isolated Incident

The adult son in our example at the beginning of this chapter is most likely an isolated incident. And let's face it, there are times when each and every one of us is so exasperated that we raise our voice. The patients we are talking about in this section are angry about a particularly frustrating situation. As discussed in Chapter 3, a person who feels "victimized" by the system, the staff, or a specific incident may display those feelings by yelling or by refusing to problem-solve with the staff.

Sometimes patients feel they have lost control of their lives, and their anger masks fear. They are afraid of not knowing the diagnosis, afraid of the diagnosis or the implications of the diagnosis, afraid of the costs or threats to their lifestyle. Parents terrified of losing their children will sometimes behave irrationally. These situations are usually isolated incidents, and are out-of-character for the patient.

Rather than being "patients from hell," these isolated-incident patients are the "patients who've been through hell," and are responding behaviorally to their experience. It can be a fine line between the patient who reacts angrily to the situation and the patient who turns his anger on the staff. Staff need to differentiate between the two—between the anger that is directed *at them* in the form of a personal attack and the anger or frustration *at the situation*—and to recognize when anger at the situation is escalating to the point that people and property are threatened.

When a patient's anger is a reaction to a specific situation, the staff need to be aware of what caused the patient's emotional outburst, and help the patient through it, using the Service Recovery protocols and guidelines. "DOGS" is an acronym for Defusing Of Grievance = Safety.[1] Larry J. Chavez, a former hostage negotiator, now with Critical Incident Associates, outlines steps to defuse an angry person that are very similar to the Service Recovery steps outlined in Chapter 2.[2]

It may be unfair to automatically label these patients as "dangerous," or "abusive," because this can exacerbate not only the current situation, but can also create a defensive environment when the patient returns at a later date for care and service.

At the same time, staff need to be sensitive to the situation escalating. If that appears to be happening, using Service Recovery protocols and calling in a supervisor immediately can help defuse the problem. This will be discussed in more detail in the section dealing with "The Abusive Patient."

▼ The Abusive Patient

There is a small group of patients who threaten the financial integrity of the organization or the safety and well-being of the staff and other patients. In this section, we discuss these three groups: the system abuser, the law-breaker, and the people abuser.

In a managed care setting, the providers have a contractual obligation to provide the patient with the care and services he or she needs. This does not mean that limits cannot be set. In some cases, the organization's providers may decide they cannot—or will not—continue to treat the patient. In these situations, the organization may be contractually responsible for making arrangements for the patient to receive care from providers not affiliated with the organization, and to pay for that care. Some situations lend themselves to a "progressive disciplinary" approach with the patient. In extreme situations, it may be necessary to terminate the enrollment contract immediately.

The System Abuser

These are the patients who abuse services to the detriment of themselves and other patients. Their behavior is not criminal, but can be disruptive and frustrating to the staff as they attempt to provide care and service to an ever-increasing number of patients with ever-decreasing resources.

Overutilizers of Services

These patients know what they want, and they badger the staff and keep chipping away until they get it. In the fee-for-service medical system, a patient sometimes requested and received services that were not always "medically necessary" because either the patient or the insurance carrier paid for them. But, in a managed care environment, there is more emphasis on ordering only those tests and doing only those procedures that are "medically necessary" or "medically indicated."

With this patient group, it is important to identify which requests to grant quickly and which requests to deny. For some staff, as soon as they hear the patient's voice, they dig in their heels and resist meeting any of the patient's requests, regardless of how reasonable they may be (recall the Annoying Patient section).

In a busy clinical setting, responding to an unending series of patient requests can be wearing, especially when resources are tight and provider time is scare. One strategy is for staff to keep in mind that patient satisfaction is important, and, if the request is not a threat to the patient (or anyone else's) well-being, and is not in direct conflict with policy, then grant the request. Staff can refer to their "solution spaces" (Chapter 2) to determine if this is something they can resolve on their own, or if other staff need to be consulted.

Often, if patients get what they ask for quickly and without a "fight," they feel more secure, and the number of requests actually decreases. This can be especially true in a managed care setting where patients sometimes feel they have to be assertive, or push hard, for what they want. Having their smaller requests met can help establish trust that will carry over when the request is for something bigger and everyone needs to be flexible.

Reducing the number of "negative" encounters can also reduce staff stress and some of the ongoing frustration of dealing with the public. But, even if the strategy does not reduce the overall number of requests, the staff have separated themselves emotionally from always opposing this demanding patient, which reduces the stress of the individual encounters.

However, chronic, serious overutilizer patients will require more specific intervention by providers and management. Habitual overutilizers can be:

- those who call the physician's office multiple times a week or day
- those who schedule appointments without following the treatment plan already developed
- those who frequently change from physician to physician and who are never satisfied with the diagnosis or treatment plan
- those who consistently request referrals to providers not affiliated with the organization
- those who are chronic pain patients (although these patients may exhibit some drug-seeking behavior, the underlying issues are often different from those who are drug abusers/chemically-dependent or those seeking to divert drugs for profit)
- those with an undiagnosed generalized anxiety disorder

One strategy is to develop a treatment and behavior contract. A patient care conference can be scheduled to include the patient's key providers (both primary care and specialty, if appropriate), a mental health services professional or hospital social worker, a manager, and a Patient Representative. In extreme cases, a spokesperson from the legal or Risk Management department may also be invited.

At the conference, the patient's medical and psychosocial status are reviewed and guidelines developed for managing the patient's care. During these meetings, it is important that the patient's perspective of what his problem is, and what he expects or needs from the providers, be included in the discussion.

After the meeting, a contract can be drafted that has specific guidelines, such as "the patient may call the nurse on Wednesday afternoon at 2:00 for a 10-minute discussion about any questions or concerns the patient may have," or "the patient is required to stay with one primary care physician for no less than six months before he can change again." The contract should be written in a way that conveys the providers' and the organization's interest in the patient's health and well-being.

Once the contract is written, the patient (and spouse, if appropriate) should be contacted to meet with the physician, a manager, and the Patient Representative to discuss the situation. Again, the meeting should be focused on the healthcare providers' interest in the patient's health and well-being. Once the contract is agreed to, and signed, by the patient, the staff must carry it out consistently, and they must be supported by management and medical staff administration.

Emergency Room Frequent Fliers

A variation of the "Overutilizer," these patients consistently use the Emergency Room for routine medical needs, the most expensive way to provide that care. Emergency Rooms may start to flag their "frequent fliers" for a review of their medical records and utilization. An appointment with the physician and/or manager to review the patient's care needs with him would then be appropriate. The physician or manager can determine if there are extenuating circumstances for the patient not coming in during regular clinic hours. The patient's primary care physician may be contacted. Working together, it may be possible to find alternatives that meet the patient's needs and are cost effective. If the patient has no primary care physician, help the patient choose one. If the patient continues to use Emergency Room services for routine care, then the physician or manager might consider the option of reviewing the record and refusing to authorize payment for the Emergency Room services that are nonurgent.

Drug Seekers

This patient group has some similarities to other System Abusers. They tend to change physicians frequently, and they often seek care episodically from Emergency Rooms.

In some managed care systems, the pharmacy can track a patient's drug use and alert the primary care physician if there seems to be unusual activity. If drug abuse is suspected, a code can be added to the patient's pharmacy information that indicates narcotics can be prescribed only with the primary care physician's authorization.

The physicians need to develop a protocol for responding to patients who exhibit drug-seeking behavior. This includes the patient who calls on Friday afternoon and insists he be given a prescription for pain medication since the physician cannot see him that day or over the weekend.

Missed Appointments

These are the patients who waste everyone's money by repeatedly not appearing for scheduled appointments. Each organization must decide for itself how many is too many, but six in a twelve-month period would certainly warrant attention from a manager.

A letter to the patient from the manager would be appropriate, a letter that identifies the problem, advises the patient of the risk to him of not changing his behavior, and offers to discuss the situation further if the patient wishes. A sample of this type of letter follows.

Missed Appointments Letter

Dear Ms. Jones:

I have been asked to write regarding several appointments made by you at Madrona Clinic which you did not keep. The time for these appointments was set aside especially for you. Missed appointments have an adverse effect on all of Madrona Medical Center's patients, particularly in the areas of increased healthcare costs and decreased appointment availability.

This kind of behavior can, in fact, jeopardize your continuing to receive care at Madrona Medical Center. The Board of Directors has adopted a policy that addresses situations like this. That policy states that not appearing for six or more appointments in a 12-month period can be grounds for requesting a patient receive medical care somewhere else.

The purpose of this letter is to express our hope that you will be able to keep the appointments you make in the future or call us in advance to cancel an appointment you will not be able to keep, which will allow us to make that time available for another patient. If you can let us know the day before (for a morning appointment) or in the morning (for an afternoon appointment), there will be adequate notice to allow scheduling of another patient, and this will not be considered a missed appointment for you.

If you wish to discuss the policy further, please feel free to call me at 555–1234. I would be more than happy to discuss it with you.

[List missed appointment dates/times at bottom of letter.]

The Law-Breaker

This section discusses patient behavior that falls into the "crimes against property" category. Unlike the "System Abuser," who can require active management, the Law-Breaker is subject to criminal prosecution if the organization chooses to pursue that course of action.

People who work in health care tend to be "helpers" or "nurturers" by nature, and their daily work usually supports that approach. They are often mentally or emotionally unprepared to deal with those who commit crimes. When these types of incidents are reported to the manager, usually after the patient has left the facility, the manager should have a policy and procedure to outline the corrective action.

Some facilities have an open-door policy, whereby service will be provided regardless of the patient's situation, such as ability to pay or behavior that is outside the "normal" limits of social acceptability. These facilities may find it difficult philosophically to develop a policy, but even they must have guidelines for when to resolve the problem directly with the patient, when to give the patient the opportunity to receive his health care somewhere else, and when to contact the police.

Misrepresentation of Identity

Occasionally, the person standing at the check-in desk is not who he says he is. The insurance identification card may have been stolen, but it is more likely that the card owner and the card user know each other. Sometimes it is an adolescent who has been in a fight and doesn't want his parents to know, and so he talks his buddy into letting him use the other's insurance card. Sometimes a young woman lets her friend use the card for a pregnancy test, or a man brings his girlfriend to the urgent care clinic and has her use his wife's card. It is not unknown for a person to have major surgery while passing himself off as somebody else.

Because medical records can follow a person for life, this misrepresentation is more complicated than a fraudulent attempt to receive free medical care. There are three issues that need to be addressed in this situation: correcting the medical record, collecting payment for services received, and deciding which authorities to notify.

Medical records staff should know how to mark the records so that the integrity of the records is maintained while correcting any misperceptions that could occur as a result of someone's else's medical information being included in the chart.

Although some people may try to bluff their way through the situation, the majority will want to pay the bill as discreetly as possible to avoid further trouble. A simple letter from a manager or administrator, such as the following, is usually all that is needed.

Misrepresentation of Identity Letter

Dear Ms. Jones,

It has come to my attention that the urine sample you brought to the clinic on [date] for a pregnancy test may have been a friend's rather than your own. If this is true, this constitutes inappropriate use of your insurance identification card to obtain services, and is fraud.

This kind of behavior can, in fact, jeopardize your continued enrollment with [organization]. The Board of Directors has adopted a policy that addresses situations like this. That policy states that misuse of the identification card may be grounds for termination of enrollment.

Please call me about this matter. If the information I was given was incorrect, we need to verify that. If the information was correct, we need to arrange for payment for this test, and for making a notation in your medical records that you were not pregnant. We also need information about the person who used your insurance card so that an accurate medical record can be started for her.

Depending on the seriousness of the incident, administration will need to decide if the card owner's insurance company and/or employer (if the person is covered by an employer group plan) should be notified.

Prescription Alteration or Forgery

Drug seekers (recall the System Abuser) will sometimes cross the line of tolerable behavior by altering prescriptions to increase the number of tablets the physician prescribed. Pharmacy staff should be alert and know what the usual protocols are for physicians writing these prescriptions. For example, the Emergency Room physicians may have a protocol that they will order only enough medication—say, 4 or 6 tablets—to last the patient until the next day when he can contact the primary care physician for additional care. If that is the usual practice, then a prescription for more than that should be verified, especially if it appears that a number has been added to change the "4 tablets" to "34 tablets" or to "40 tablets."

If a prescription alteration is suspected, the pharmacy should notify the Patient Representative or Administration immediately. Depending on the severity of the alteration and the patient's history with the organization, a warning letter from an administrator such as the following may be appropriate.

Alteration of Prescription Letter

Dear Ms. Jones,

It has come to my attention that the prescription given to you by Dr. Smith in the Emergency Room on (date) was altered from 10 Tylenol with codeine tablets to 40 tablets. The pharmacists recognized the alteration and verified with the Emergency Room staff that only 10 tablets had been authorized for your prescription. I am writing to advise you that altering prescriptions is not acceptable for any reason.

This kind of behavior can also jeopardize your continued enrollment with [organization]. The Board of Directors has adopted a policy that addresses situations like this. That policy states that alteration or forgery of prescriptions may be grounds for termination of enrollment.

Although this incident will not be reviewed further, I felt it important to advise you of the existence of this policy. If you wish to discuss the incident or the policy with me further, please feel free to call me at 555–1234. I would be more than happy to discuss it with you.

Prescription forgery on stolen forms is a criminal offense that needs to be documented and addressed. In some cases, Administration will handle the situation directly; in other cases, the police will be notified to take the necessary action. Prescription alteration or forgery should be considered grounds for immediate termination of enrollment with the organization or denial of routine medical care in the future, even if the behavior did not threaten the safety and well-being of staff or other patients.

The People Abuser

What goes on in the community around the medical facility will be represented in the patient population. If verbal and physical abuse occur in surrounding homes and business establishments, it will occur in hospitals and clinics.

The Department of Justice estimates that one in four workers are attacked, threatened, or harassed each year, with verbal violence occuring six times more often than physical violence. Those who threaten, harass, and attack are usually white males over 30, and two thirds are "strangers," such as in a robbery, or customers. Those at greatest risk are staff with high public contact, especially in businesses where good customer service is not considered important.[3]

The true "patient from hell" is the patient who consistently harasses staff. Despite the historic tolerance of healthcare workers, there are lines of behavior that should not be crossed, both verbal and physical abuse that staff should not be subjected to, or expected to endure. Management has a responsibility to patients to maintain a safe environment to receive care and services. Management has an equally strong responsibility to maintain a safe environment for the staff who provide those services.

It is often difficult to comprehend why patients (or family members) treat staff so shabbily. Healthcare workers are there to help patients and their families. The staff are usually very caring people. So why does the abuse occur? Five factors have been identified that may contribute to a better understanding of this disruptive and unacceptable behavior.[4]

The first factor is that patients fear loss of freedom. It does not matter how minor the medical condition may be; the patient finds himself in an alien environment with people who speak a strange language. The patient's clothes are removed, his personal belongings may be bagged and taken somewhere else for "safe keeping," and his family members are asked to wait outside the room. He may fear the future: future disability, future financial solvency, future disfigurement. The patient may see fighting back as the only way to regain some of that loss of freedom.

The second factor is the patient's expectation for attention and the behaviors he knows will give him the attention he wants. He has learned that acting out will bring faster service elsewhere, and so he expects to have the same result in the ER or clinic. His assaultive behavior may actually increase because he sees himself as less accountable because "he is sick."

The third factor is that these patients often see staff as part of the environment. As they depersonalize the individual staff member, their own self-control decreases because they are not yelling or hitting a "real" person.

The fourth factor is the mindset of certain segments of the male population that see women as subservient. In a field that has a high percentage of women employees and managers, this can result in a patient who is abusive toward the receptionist and nurse, but is a model of decorum when meeting with a male physician.

The fifth factor is the American value that hospitals are there to take care of anyone, and a resulting provider attitude that is more tolerant of abusive behavior.

Any of these factors, or any combination of factors, can threaten the well-being of staff and other patients with a patient's disruptive, and sometimes dangerous, behavior. The behavior falls into two main categories: behavior that can be changed by working with the patient to establish guidelines for acceptable behavior, and behavior that is grounds for immediate termination of enrollment from the managed care plan, refusal to provide future care (except for life-threatening emergencies), and possibly criminal action.

Some patients are verbally abusive because they have found it results in faster service. Maybe they enjoy being the bully, watching others scurry out of their way. Often, though, when someone challenges their behavior and declares it is unacceptable and will no longer be tolerated, the patient backs down and agrees to act more appropriately. The following are a few of the types who fall into this category.

Screamers

Some patients attempt to get their way by screaming or having a "temper tantrum" in the waiting room. Adults not under the influence of drugs or alcohol have been known to throw themselves on the floor, kicking and screaming, until staff agree to do what the patient wants. The fastest way to defuse the situation is to get the patient out of the public area and into an exam room or office. Once there is no audience, the patient will often settle down. In extreme cases, it may be necessary to call for security or police assistance (criteria for police intervention is discussed further in the "violent patient" section of this chapter).

The Know-It-All's

These are the patients who are certain they know how the system works and know what service they want, when they want it, how they want it delivered, and by whom. Anyone who attempts to explain how the system really works, or who says they cannot have exactly what they have requested, is "stupid," or an "incompetent jerk."

These patients, who tend to be younger, can be verbally brutal to front-line staff who the Know-It-All's perceive as being powerless or obstructionist, or simply too stupid to know what to do. One strategy is to transfer these patients to a supervisor or manager early in the conversation. A supervisor can set limits by telling the patient that a particular behavior is not acceptable. When these patients deal with someone *they* perceive as being in authority, they often back down and begin to listen to other options.

The Verbally Abusive

These patients are usually older men, but sometimes they are highly stressed professional women. They try to bully their way through the system, using their size or loud voice to intimidate front-line staff. They may swear and call the staff names. They may refuse to give their name or state their problem, but demand to be put through to the physician immediately. They can also be chameleonlike in behavior by showing great respect to physicians, managers, or others whom they believe have the authority to get them what they want.

Managers must take steps to prevent the victimization of front-line staff. Contacting the patient with a warning letter lets the patient know someone is paying attention to their behavior. It also avoids a confrontation in which the patient feels he must save-face and defend himself, usually making the problem worse. If the patient does not like the letter, he has a choice: he can seek future medical care somewhere else.

The warning letter includes a basic statement of the problem situation, a statement about the potential impact of that situation, and a concluding paragraph that identifies what action the manager is taking and offers the opportunity to discuss the situation further. In these cases, a letter from the manager, such as the following, may be appropriate to send to the patient.

Verbal Abuse of Staff—Example 1

Dear Mr. Jones:

I am writing to follow up your telephone conversation with our OB/GYN department on [date]. The receptionist reported that you wanted to cancel your wife's appointment with Dr. Smith and have her receive her care at our Madrona Clinic instead. When the receptionist tried to explain how to do this, you reportedly became very angry, including making threats to sue the staff if anything is wrong with your wife. I am writing to advise you that verbal abuse and harassment of the staff is not acceptable for any reason.

This kind of behavior can, in fact, jeopardize your continuing to receive care at [name of organization]. The Board of Directors has adopted a policy that addresses situations like this. That policy states that verbal abuse and harassment of [organization's] staff and other patients may be grounds for termination of enrollment.

If you have questions or concerns about your wife's care, I recommend you contact her physicians and their staff to work *with* them, rather than be confrontational. A copy of this letter has been filed in your chart. If you wish to discuss the incident or the policy with me further, please feel free to call me at 555–1234. I would be more than happy to discuss it with you.

Verbal Abuse of Staff—Example 2

Dear Ms. Jones:

It has come to my attention that on [date] you became upset when told your husband's insurance coverage would not begin until [date]. You reportedly became verbally abusive to the admitting clerk, including swearing at her. I am writing to advise you that yelling and swearing at the staff is not acceptable for any reason.

This kind of behavior can, in fact, jeopardize your continuing to receive care at [name of organization]. The Board of Directors has adopted a policy that addresses situations like this. That policy states that verbal abuse and harassment of [organization's] staff and other patients may be grounds for termination of enrollment.

Although this incident will not be reviewed further, I felt it important to advise you of the existence of this policy. A copy of this letter has been filed in your chart. If you wish to discuss the incident or the policy with me further, please feel free to call me at 555–1234. I would be more than happy to discuss it with you.

Verbal Abuse of Staff—Example 3

Dear Mr. Jones:

It has come to my attention that on [date] you became upset about the length of time you had to wait for your appointment. While you were angry, you reportedly became verbally abusive to the staff and deliberately tipped over a potted plant. I am writing to advise you that yelling at the staff and destroying property is not acceptable for any reason.

This kind of behavior can, in fact, jeopardize your continuing to receive care at [name of organization]. The Board of Directors has adopted a policy that addresses situations like this. That policy states that verbal abuse and harassment of [organization's] staff and other patients and damage to property may be grounds for termination of enrollment.

If you become dissatisfied with services in the future, please contact me, the department manager, or the patient representative department rather than taking it out on the staff or damaging property. A copy of this letter has been filed in your chart. If you wish to discuss the incident or the policy with me further, please feel free to call me at 555–1234. I would be more than happy to discuss it with you.

If the verbal abuse does not stop after a warning letter is sent, then a face-to-face meeting between the patient, a physician, a manager or administrator, and the Patient Representative is sometimes needed to reinforce that the organization is serious about the issue and to clearly establish behavior boundaries. Part of the contract may be that if the patient is dissatisfied with any aspect of care or service, he is to call the manager directly, and not discuss it with front-line staff.

Sexual Harassment

There are patients, both inpatient and outpatient, who will make sexual comments or gestures to staff or other patients. This can include exposing themselves "accidentally," asking the nurse to touch the genitals, references to the aide's sexuality, and other lewd comments or suggestions.

Even if there is no physical contact, this type of behavior is unacceptable. Staff should be encouraged to report the behavior to their supervisor immediately, and know that the supervisor will take action.

If the patient is still in the hospital, an administrator should follow up with the patient and make it very clear that such behavior will not be tolerated, and could be grounds for termination of enrollment in the managed care plan or refusal to provide future medical care.

If the patient has left the building, an administrator should contact the patient, preferably in writing using a letter such as the one that follows.

Sexual Harassment—No Physical Contact Letter

Dear Mr. Jones:

It has come to my attention that on [date], you were accused of making sexual advances toward another patient. She has indicated she will not pursue the matter by contacting the police. However, I am writing to advise you that harassment of the staff and other patients is not acceptable.

[**OR**] It has come to my attention that while you were in the clinic on [date] to see Dr. Smith, you made inappropriate comments to his medical assistant. I am writing to advise you that sexual harassment is not acceptable.

This kind of behavior can jeopardize your continuing to receive care with [organization]. The Board of Directors has adopted a policy that addresses situations like this. That policy states that sexual harassment of staff or other patients may be grounds for termination of enrollment.

I felt it important to advise you of the existence of this policy. Although this incident has been documented and a copy of this letter filed in your chart, it will not be reviewed further. If you wish to discuss the incident or the policy with me further, please feel free to call me at 555–1234. I would be more than happy to discuss it with you.

Threats That DO NOT Cause Reasonable Fear of Immediate Harm

A patient stood before the manager's desk, yelling and threatening all the things he was going to do. On another occasion, the manager might have been concerned, but this time she wasn't. She took her cue from the man's four-year-old daughter who played quietly at his feet and occasionally tugged on his pant leg and asked daddy to look at the picture she was coloring.

A lot of people vent their frustrations with a lot of arm-waving and idle threats. They do not mean anything by it, and those around them all the time know that. But just because they don't intend to follow through with their threats does not mean their barrage isn't unsettling to the staff and other patients within hearing distance and disruptive to the caring, healing atmosphere the staff is attempting to foster.

Again, a letter from an administrator, such as the one that follows, can serve to document that a warning was given. Offering to meet indicates a willingness to work with the patient. But, such behavior should not be allowed to continue.

Threats of Violence (No Fear of Harm) Letter

Dear Mr. Jones:

It has come to my attention that on [date], you became angry about the wait for lab results and threatened the staff with bodily harm if they did not produce the information you wanted immediately. I am writing to advise you that threatening the staff is not acceptable behavior for any reason.

This kind of behavior can, in fact, jeopardize your continuing to receive medical care at [organization]. The Board of Directors has adopted a policy that addresses situations like this. That policy states that verbal abuse and harassment of the staff can be grounds for termination of services.

Although this incident will not be reviewed further, I felt it important to advise you of the existence of this policy. A copy of this letter has been filed in your chart. If you become dissatisfied with services in the future, please contact me, the department manager, or the patient representative rather than taking your frustration out on the staff.

Behavior Requiring Immediate Action

Ours is a violent society, and healthcare providers treat the victims every day. Regrettably, that violence is spilling over into the clinical setting, with staff becoming the victims. In July 1998, the Bureau of Justice reported that between 1992 and 1996, physicians experienced 10,000 nonfatal assaults; nurses experienced 69,500, and those were the reported and documented assaults. The organization Nurse Advocate believes nurses either minimize or ignore violence against themselves, or fail to report incidents because they fear retaliation or because they believe employers are unsupportive.

The Center for Disease Control (CDC) has called workplace violence a "national epidemic." The CDC's National Institute for Occupational Safety and Health division adopted a policy statement on the need for every business to have a violence-prevention program and policy.[5]

A 1999 Gallup poll showed that nationwide, 20% of Americans who work outside the home were "somewhat worried" to "very worried" about a co-worker committing an act of violence, and 18% reportedly knew someone they felt capable of committing an act of violence in the workplace.[6]

This means everyone must take steps to prevent incidents of abuse and future abuse.

It means staff must take the time to document and report incidents of abusive patient behavior.

It means managers must follow up on staff reports of abusive patient behavior by confronting the patient and setting limits.

It means administrators must support their employees, even if it means refusing to treat the patient any longer and/or filing criminal charges against the patient.

Homicide is the third-leading cause of death in the workplace, and the leading cause of fatal occupational injuries among women. The State of California's OSHA studied why the number of incidents of death and serious injury were increasing for healthcare workers. According to a 1998 report, public exposure may be an important risk, and that risk is increased "particularly in emotionally charged situations with mentally disturbed persons or when workers appear to be unprotected."[7]

There should be zero tolerance for three types of patient behavior:

- Threats that cause an employee, visitor, or other patient to have a reasonable fear of immediate bodily harm;

- Dangerous, disruptive, or antisocial behavior that threatens the safety of staff, visitors, or other patients, or that jeopardizes the safe operation of the facility;

- Nonconsensual physical contact with aggressive or sexual overtones toward facility staff, visitors, or other patients.

Administration should assume responsibility for developing policies and procedures to prevent and respond to these incidents. These plans and preparations are as important as traditional disaster planning.

In addition to developing policies and procedures, local law enforcement should be invited to meet with staff to discuss concerns and potential scenarios, and to provide some basic self-defense training to staff. Clinic and hospital staff should learn body positioning techniques to prevent escalation of a volatile situation. Those who make home visits need training in how to assess their safety using "compliance indicators" before visiting a home for the first time, how to establish a buddy system with someone in the main office, and other tips for protecting themselves while working in the field.

Sometimes modifications will be suggested for the building, such as:

- Installing highly visible cameras. Many abusive people do not want their actions taped.
- Raising reception desks so front-desk staff can look directly at patients, rather than up.
- Auto-dial alarms or panic buttons to trigger a police response.

In some cases, police intervention may be required, with staff relinquishing all responsibility for the situation to the police immediately. Staff need to know what the guidelines are for contacting the police and be comfortable with these guidelines before a crisis occurs. They also need to know that if they call 911, they will not be reprimanded by an administrator later.

In other cases, however, staff may need to take preliminary action because law enforcement personnel are not yet on the premises, or because the situation has not escalated to the point that the police are contacted. When this occurs, staff need to have procedures in place that they can follow. Some staff will require additional training on how to deal with the situation before the police are contacted and/or arrive. The following are some suggestions to consider when developing a plan.

The Policy

The organization should establish a policy to address situations involving people who physically assault or verbally threaten bodily harm to staff, other patients, or visitors in the facility, or who destroy, or threaten to destroy, property—*before* an incident occurs.

The organization should also have a policy included in its employee and patient orientation materials that prohibits the possession of a weapon, including aerosol sprays:

- by any patient, staff, or visitor, with the exception of law enforcement personnel while on professional business,
- while on property owned, leased, or otherwise controlled by the organization.

The Procedure

To implement the policy, staff will need clear procedures they can follow quickly and easily in a crisis. The procedures should include instructions on how to control or contain a person who becomes physically or verbally assaultive, as well as what steps Administration will take after the initial crisis.

Staff should be encouraged to use their instincts and best judgment when deciding that the procedures need to be implemented. If different scenarios have been discussed in staff meetings, the staff can often recognize when a situation is intensifying and take steps to contain it before it escalates out of control. The "Solution Space" approach can be useful here (see Figure 2-1 page 11).

Implementing the Procedure

Staff should know that in a life-threatening situation they should not hesitate to call 911. In other circumstances, it may be better for staff to contact the in-house "crisis team" to assist with the problem.

The Crisis Team

One strategy for dealing with potentially violent or escalating situations is for each clinic or facility to form a special team specifically trained in crisis intervention. These teams should be available during all normal facility hours (back-up members will be needed). They should include a minimum of five people representing different services, and be of mixed gender and physical size.

The first team member to respond will usually assume responsibility for directing the team. The team leader should be competent and confident in his or her ability to communicate with the patient, should know the patient involved, and/or the situation. If communication between the team leader and the patient deteriorates to the point that violence is again a strong possibility, it should be understood that another team member will assume the leadership role and be the person who communicates with the patient.

The Team Leader

This person is responsible for assessing the situation and developing the team's action plan. A supportive approach to responding to the patient would include nonthreatening body language, calmly setting limits, and demonstrating a supportive, concerned attitude. A more direct approach would be to set clear limits with specific consequences if the patient does not comply.

The team leader is responsible for:

- requesting police intervention if immediate intervention is required
- giving clear and specific instructions to team members, such as to implement the evacuation plan or to restrict access to the area
- communicating with the patient
- preparing the facility and staff for the patient's arrival if the threats were made by phone
- obtaining background medical and mental health information about the patient, if appropriate.

After the Incident

Depending on the situation, arrangements need to be made to provide the patient with future care, either at the organization's facilities, or at facilities not affiliated with the organization. Termination of enrollment from the organization or managed care plan may also be a consideration, depending on the gravity of the incident.

Those staff, other patients, and visitors who were present or involved in the incident should be interviewed and/or asked to put their perspectives in writing. The team members and the involved staff should also have a group debriefing session to review what precipitated the incident, and how well the crisis intervention process worked (similar to a disaster drill review).

Within three working days of the incident, a final report should be written by the team leader for Administration that includes:

- the written statements of staff, visitors, and other patients
- a summary of the debriefing session
- recommendations for further actions, including possible system changes, training needs for crisis intervention situations, and follow-up action with the patient.

At this point it may be appropriate to involve the Patient Representative, especially if follow-up action with the patient is needed. These actions may include:

- requiring the patient change physicians and/or facilities
- a warning that such incidents can result in termination of enrollment
- a behavioral contract with the patient for future interaction with the organization's staff
- termination of enrollment from the managed care plan or organization, either with 60 days advance notice or effective immediately, depending on the nature of the incident.

These actions should be decided on by Administration within three days of receiving the final report from the crisis intervention team leader.

No one wants to be in a potentially dangerous situation. Yet workplace violence is a reality in today's society, more common than the fires, chemical spills, and earthquakes prepared for in disaster planning.

Administration must send a clear message that, regardless of the perceived provocation, patients have a responsibility to treat staff and other patients with the same level of respect and dignity that they expect to receive.

NOTES

1. Sheryl and Don Grimme, "Violence in the Workplace: The Realities and the Options," <www.businessknowhow.com/manage/violwork.htm>

2. Larry J. Chavez, BA, MPA, www.workplace-violence.com.

3. Sheryl and Don Grimme, "Violence in the Workplace: The Realities and the Options," <www.ghr-training.com>.

4. Interview with Ken Bayne, Empire Health Services, August 13, 1999.

5. National Institute for Occupational Safety and Health, "Developing and Implementing a Workplace Violence Prevention Program and Policy," July 16, 1996, <www.cdc.gov/niosh/violdev.html>.

6. Gallup Organization, "Poll Releases," August 6, 1999.

7. State of California CAL/OSHA, "Guidelines for Security and Safety of Health Care and Community Service Workers," published to html on Tuesday, March 10, 1998. <www.dir.ca.gov\dosh\dosh_publications\hcworker.html>.

Appendix A

Service Recovery Protocols for Medical Receptionists

Service Recovery, as described in Chapter 2, involves five basic steps. The following is a model for developing Service Recovery protocols for medical receptionists, as well as examples of scripting for problems received by front-line staff in physician offices and clinics.

Model

I. Patient/Customer Contact

    A. Listen—focus on the patient/customer with attentive body language (if in person) and voice inflections (if over the telephone)

    B. Ask open-ended questions

    C. Empathize; validate the patient/customer's perspective

    D. Clarify the patient/customer's expectation for resolution

II. Acknowledge

    A. Apologize—without assigning blame or guilt

    B. Verify the facts

    C. Explain what you can do; provide general overview of the process you will follow to resolve the concern

    D. Agree on next contact. For instance, "I'm going to look into this for you and get back to you [time frame]"—hopefully in 24 hours/up to 48 hours

III. Problem Solve

    A. Consult with others

        1. Exchange information

        2. Collect information for explaining resolution

        3. Identify options

        4. Together, ask what's the right thing to do; what can we do; what will we do

    B. Explore options

        1. Identify options

        2. Together, ask what's the right thing to do; what can we do; what will we do

    C. Update consumer if necessary

IV. Respond/Refer

    A. Contact patient/customer with customized resolution

    B. Transfer complaint, if appropriate, to another department/division/region etc.

        1. Contact the resource person and relay all the pertinent information and facts about the problem

        2. Negotiate with the resource person to assume responsibility for investigating, reviewing, and/or resolving the problem; determine who will notify the patient/customer with the final resolution

        3. Advise the patient/customer of the next step, including who the resource person is and how to reach him or her

        4. Document in writing the pertinent facts and the plan for resolution, and send a copy to the resource person

    C. Update patient/customer if necessary

V. Follow-Up

    A. Bring closure to complaint
Summarize patient/customer's request, the actions you took, and agreed-upon resolution

    B. Thank patient/customer

    C. Share your organization's Service Recovery standards, if appropriate:

        1. You strive to recognize the patient/customer as an individual

        2. You strive to provide the patient/customer with an easy, obvious process for sharing concerns

        3. You strive to provide the patient/customer with a key contact person

        4. You strive for a fair resolution

        5. You strive for a fast resolution

        6. You strive to provide consistent, clear, and accurate information

D. Written follow-up letter

1. Summarize patient/customer's request, the actions you took, and agreed-upon resolution

2. Apologize for the patient/customer's feelings of dissatisfaction or inconvenience

3. Report any system changes that have occurred as a result of this complaint

4. Offer to assist in the future if needed

E. Document complaint and distribute, if appropriate

Service Recovery Standards

85% of all complaints are resolved by the person who hears the complaint

85% of all complaints are resolved the same day

Complex complaints are resolved within two weeks

Have receptionists identify the complaints they hear most often. The following are ideas for how receptionists can respond to those complaints using Service Recovery protocols. The protocols can be modified to meet the needs of the particular office, facility, or hospital, or they can be used as examples for training purposes. Note that not all patient problems require all five Service Recovery steps.

▼ Medical Receptionist

Appointment Wait Time for Own Primary Care Practice

I. Patient/Customer Contact

A. Listen—focus on the patient/customer with attentive body language (if in person) and voice inflections (if over the telephone)

B. Ask open-ended questions

1. "What is your concern about waiting until _____?" (ask only if it's not clear why patient/customer can't wait—do not antagonize the patient/customer further)

2. "I'm sorry. I don't understand why you think you need an earlier appointment. Can you help me understand?"

C. Empathize; validate the patient/customer's perspective

1. "I'm glad you let me know that this is not a good time for you."

2. "I understand you are frustrated by this."

3. "It sounds like you're really worried about these symptoms."

D. Clarify expectation for resolution

1. "When did you want to be seen?"

2. "When are you available—are there any times you cannot come for an appointment?"

II. Acknowledge

    A. Apologize—without assigning blame or guilt

        1. "I'm sorry this isn't a convenient time for you."

        2. "I'm sorry Dr. _____ doesn't have an earlier appointment for a physical exam."

    B. Verify the facts:
       "Let me make sure I understand what you've told me."

    C. Explain what you can do; provide general overview of the process you will follow to resolve the concern

        1. Offer earlier appointment if you can;
          offer to put on cancellation list;
          offer appointment with PA or another MD

        2. "I'm going to talk to _____ , Dr. _____ 's nurse, about your concerns and ask her to call you back. (She may want to pull your chart and review it with Dr. _____ first.)"

    D. Agree on next contact

        1. "I'm going to ask [nurse] to call you back today. If you don't hear from her by [time frame], please call me. Where can she reach you? Is there any time you won't be available at that number?"

III. Problem Solve
   Consult with others—contact RN to

        1. Exchange information

        2. Identify options not already offered to patient/customer

        3. Together, ask what's the right thing to do; what can we do; what will we do

IV. Respond/Refer

    A. Transfer complaint, if appropriate, to RN to contact patient

        1. Contact the resource person, and relay all the pertinent information and facts about the problem

        2. Negotiate with the resource person to assume responsibility for investigating, reviewing, and/or resolving the problem; determine who will notify the patient/customer with the final resolution

        3. Advise the patient/customer of the next step, including who the resource person is and how to reach him or her

        4. Document in writing the pertinent facts and the plan for resolution, and send a copy to the resource person

V. Follow-Up

   A. Bring closure to complaint
      "I'm calling to follow up with you about the time of your appointment. How will [day], [date], [time] work for you?"

   B. Thank patient/customer
      "Thank you for letting me help you with this."

   C. Share your organization's Service Recovery standards, if appropriate:

      1. You strive to recognize the patient/customer as an individual

      2. You strive to provide the patient/customer with an easy, obvious process for sharing concerns

      3. You strive to provide the patient/customer with a key contact person

      4. You strive for a fair resolution

      5. You strive for a fast resolution

      6. You strive to provide consistent, clear, and accurate information

   D. Written follow-up letter

      1. Summarize patient/customer's request, the actions you took, and agreed-upon resolution

      2. Apologize for the patient/customer's feelings of dissatisfaction or inconvenience

      3. Report any system changes that have occurred as a result of this complaint

      4. Offer to assist in the future if needed

   E. Document complaint and distribute, if appropriate

▼ Medical Receptionist

Appointment Wait Time for Specialist

I. Patient/Customer Contact

   A. Listen—focus on the patient/customer with attentive body language (if in person) and voice inflections (if over the telephone)

   B. Empathize; validate the patient/customer's perspective

      1. "I'm glad you let me know that this is not a good time for you."

      2. "I understand you are frustrated by this."

      3. "It sounds like you're really worried about these symptoms."

   C. Clarify expectation for resolution

1. "When did you want to be seen?"

2. "When are you available—are there any times you cannot come for an appointment?"

II. Acknowledge

A. Apologize—without assigning blame or guilt

1. "I'm sorry this isn't a convenient time for you."

2. "I'm sorry [specialty department] didn't offer you an earlier appointment."

B. Verify the facts

"Let me make sure I understand what you've told me."

C. Explain what you can do; provide general overview of the process you will follow to resolve the concern

"I'm going to talk to _____, Dr. _____'s nurse about your concerns and ask her to call you back. (She may want to pull your chart and review it with Dr. _____ first.)"

D. Agree on next contact

"I'm going to ask [nurse] to call you back today. If you don't hear from her by [time frame], please call me. Where can she reach you? Is there any time you won't be available at that number?"

III. Respond/Refer

A. Consult with others—contact RN to transfer complaint to her

1. Contact the resource person and relay all the pertinent information and facts about the problem

2. Negotiate with the resource person to assume responsibility for investigating, reviewing, and/or resolving the problem; determine who will notify the patient/customer with the final resolution

3. Advise the patient/customer of the next step, including who the resource person is and how to reach him or her

4. Document in writing the pertinent facts and the plan for resolution, and send a copy to the resource person

IV. Follow-Up

Thank patient/customer

"Thank you for letting me help you with this."

B. Share your organization's Service Recovery standards, if appropriate

1. You strive to recognize the patient/customer as an individual

2. You strive to provide the patient/customer with an easy, obvious process for sharing concerns

3. You strive to provide the patient/customer with a key contact person

4. You strive for a fair resolution

5. You strive for a fast resolution

6. You strive to provide consistent, clear, and accurate information

C. Written follow-up letter

1. Summarize patient/customer's request, the actions you took, and agreed-upon resolution

2. Apologize for the patient/customer's feelings of dissatisfaction or inconvenience

3. Report any system changes that have occurred as a result of this complaint

4. Offer to assist in the future if needed

D. Document complaint and distribute, if appropriate

▼ Medical Receptionist

Staff Attitude

I. Patient/Customer Contact

A. Listen—focus on the patient/customer with attentive body language (if in person) and voice inflections (if over the telephone)

B. Ask open-ended questions

1. "Who said this to you? When?"

2. "What specifically did he [or she] say?"

3. "Can you describe the encounter [or situation] in more detail for me?"

C. Empathize; validate the patient/customer's perspective

1. "It sounds like that was a difficult [awkward/frustrating] situation for you."

II. Acknowledge

A. Apologize—without assigning blame or guilt

1. "I'm sorry you felt _____ ."

2. "I'm sure it wasn't their intent to _____ ."

B. Verify the facts
"Let me make sure I understand what you've told me."

C. Explain what you can do; provide general overview of the process you will follow to resolve the concern
"I will document your complaint and share it with our Patient Representative. She will follow up from there."

D. Clarify expectation for resolution

1. "Is there anything else you would like done?"

   a. Change primary care physician—transfer patient to Physician Selection

   b. Second opinion appointment—make appointment within office or transfer caller to the appropriate section or office for appointment scheduling (give other receptionist some background as to what patient needs so patient doesn't have to repeat story or get caught in bureaucracy)

   c. Other expectations for resolution—refer to Patient Representative

      • Contact the Patient Representative and relay all the pertinent information and facts about the problem

      • Negotiate with the Patient Representative to assume responsibility for investigating, reviewing, and/or resolving the problem; determine who will notify the patient/customer with the final resolution

      • Advise the patient/customer of the next step, including who the Patient Representative is and how to reach him or her

      • Document in writing the pertinent facts and the plan for resolution, and send a copy to the Patient Representative

      • If requested resolution is refund of co-pay, then office/department/division should have a developed process for doing this efficiently

      • If requested resolution is payment of bill for non-Plan services, then request copy of bills (itemized with procedure codes) and non-Plan records

E. Agree on next contact

1. "I'm going to document this and send it to our Patient Representative. Would you like to talk to her, too? When can you be reached? Where?"

2. "I'm going to transfer you to Physician Selection [the _____ department/office] to change physicians [schedule an appointment]."

III. Follow-Up

A. Bring closure to complaint
   Summarize patient/customer's request, the actions you took, and agreed-upon resolution

B. Thank consumer

C. Share your organization's Service Recovery standards, if appropriate

1. You strive to recognize the patient/customer as an individual

2. You strive to provide the patient/customer with an easy, obvious process for sharing concerns

3. You strive to provide the patient/customer with a key contact person

4. You strive for a fair resolution

5. You strive for a fast resolution

6. You strive to provide consistent, clear, and accurate information

D. Written follow-up letter

1. Summarize patient/customer's request, the actions you took, and agreed-upon resolution

2. Apologize for the patient/customer's feelings of dissatisfaction or inconvenience

3. Report any system changes that have occurred as a result of this complaint

4. Offer to assist in the future if needed

E. Document complaint and distribute, as appropriate

▼ Medical Receptionist
Access to Own Primary Care Physician

I. Patient/Customer Contact

A. Listen—focus on the patient/customer with attentive body language (if in person) and voice inflections (if over the telephone)

B. Ask open-ended questions

1. "When was the last time you saw Dr. _____ ?"

2. "Who have you seen for this problem already?"

C. Empathize; validate the patient/customer's perspective

1. "I understand how frustrated you are."

2. "I'm glad you let me know how important an appointment with Dr. _____ is to you."

D. Clarify expectation for resolution
"When do you need to be seen? Do you feel this is an urgent problem, or can it wait until Dr. _____ returns?"

II. Acknowledge

A. Apologize—without assigning blame or guilt
"I'm sorry this isn't what you were expecting."

B. Verify the facts:
"Let me make sure I understand what you've told me."

C. Explain what you can do; provide general overview of the process you will follow to resolve the concern

1. "I understand you want an appointment with Dr. _____ . He[she] is out of the office until _____ ; I can either schedule you for that day, or, if you need to be seen earlier, I can offer you an appointment with Dr./PA _____ ."

2. "I will document your concern and share it with our chief of staff, as he reviews the physicians' schedules."

3. "Dr. _____ recently assumed extra administrative responsibilities, so he has fewer appointments available. Perhaps you would like to consider changing to a physician who has a full-time practice."

4. "Dr. _____ is part of a shared practice, so he [she] is only in the office half time. Perhaps you would like to consider changing to a physician who has a full-time practice."

D. Agree on next contact

"I'm going to document this complaint. Here is the number if you decide you want to change physicians. If you decide you want an earlier appointment with another physician for this problem, please let me know."

III. Problem Solve

A. Consult with others—share complaint with Patient Representative

B. Update patient/customer if necessary

IV. Respond/Refer

A. Contact patient/customer with customized resolution

B. Transfer complaint, if appropriate, to chief of staff or to Patient Representative

1. Contact the resource person and relay all the pertinent information and facts about the problem

2. Negotiate with the resource person to assume responsibility for investigating, reviewing, and/or resolving the problem; determine who will notify the patient/customer with the final resolution

3. Advise the patient/customer of the next step, including who the resource person is and how to reach him or her

4. Document in writing the pertinent facts and the plan for resolution, and send a copy to the resource person

C. Update patient/customer if necessary

V. Follow-Up

A. Bring closure to complaint

Summarize patient/customer's request, the actions you took, and agreed-upon resolution

B. Thank patient/customer

"Thank you for sharing this concern with me. We want you to be satisfied with the service you receive here."

C. Share your organization's Service Recovery standards, if appropriate

1. You strive to recognize the patient/customer as an individual

2. You strive to provide the patient/customer with an easy, obvious process for sharing concerns

3. You strive to provide the patient/customer with a key contact person

4. You strive for a fair resolution

5. You strive for a fast resolution

6. You strive to provide consistent, clear, and accurate information

D. Written follow-up letter

1. Summarize patient/customer's request, the actions you took, and agreed-upon resolution

2. Apologize for the patient/customer's feelings of dissatisfaction or inconvenience

3. Report any system changes that have occurred as a result of this complaint

4. Offer to assist in the future if needed

E. Document complaint and distribute, if appropriate

▼ Medical Receptionist

Mid-Level Practitioner Appointment, Not MD Appointment

I. Patient/Customer Contact

A. Listen—focus on the patient/customer with attentive body language (if in person) and voice inflections (if over the telephone)

B. Ask open-ended questions

1. "Could you tell me your concerns about seeing a physician assistant [nurse practitioner]?"

2. "When was the last time you saw Dr. _____?"

3. "Who have you seen for this problem already?"

C. Empathize; validate the patient/customer's perspective

1. "It sounds like you would prefer to see an MD rather than a physician assistant [nurse practitioner]."

2. "It sounds like you are really worried about these symptoms."

3. "I understand you are frustrated by this."

D. Clarify expectation for resolution

"When do you need to be seen? Do you feel this is an urgent problem, or can it wait until Dr. _____ is available?"

II. Acknowledge

A. Apologize—without assigning blame or guilt

1. "I'm sorry you can't [didn't] see the provider you expected to see."

2. "I'm sorry a physician appointment wasn't [isn't] available at a time that was [is] convenient for you."

      3. "I'm sorry Dr. _____ doesn't have an earlier appointment for this problem."

  B. Verify the facts

III. Problem Solve

  A. Explore options

      1. "I'd be happy to assist you in scheduling an appointment with a physician."

      2. "When did you want to be seen?"

      3. "When are you available—are there any times you cannot come for an appointment?"

      4. "Would you be willing to go to another Plan facility in _____ or _____?"

  B. Provide information and explain/educate—background and training of physician assistants [nurse practitioners], how they are used, etc.

  C. Verify that patient/customer still insists on seeing MD, even after explanation of PA's [NP's] scope of practice

IV. Respond/Refer

  A. Contact consumer with customized resolution
    "I have contacted Dr. _____'s office, and you have an appointment
    at _____ on _____."

  B. Transfer complaint, if appropriate, to a physician's office for assistance in scheduling the appointment

      1. Contact the resource person and relay all the pertinent information and facts about the problem

      2. Negotiate with the resource person to assume responsibility for investigating, reviewing, and/or resolving the problem; determine who will notify the patient/customer with the final resolution

      3. Advise the patient/customer of the next step, including who the resource person is and how to reach him or her. Then, transfer consumer to MD's office for assistance with scheduling **after** advising consumer to call you back if there are any further difficulties.

      4. Document in writing the pertinent facts and the plan for resolution, and send a copy to the resource person

V. Follow-Up

  A. Bring closure to complaint
    Summarize patient/customer's request, the actions you took, and agreed-upon resolution

  B. Thank patient/customer

C. Share your organization's Service Recovery standards, if appropriate

1. You strive to recognize the patient/customer as an individual

2. You strive to provide the patient/customer with an easy, obvious process for sharing concerns

3. You strive to provide the patient/customer with a key contact person

4. You strive for a fair resolution

5. You strive for a fast resolution

6. You strive to provide consistent, clear, and accurate information

D. Written follow-up letter

1. Summarize patient/customer's request, the actions you took, and agreed-upon resolution

2. Apologize for the patient/customer's feelings of dissatisfaction or inconvenience

3. Report any system changes that have occurred as a result of this complaint

4. Offer to assist in the future if needed

E. Document complaint and distribute, if appropriate

▼ Medical Receptionist

Pharmacy Wait

I. Patient/Customer Contact

A. Listen—focus on the patient/customer with attentive body language (if in person) and voice inflections (if over the telephone)

B. Ask open-ended questions

1. "Was this a new prescription or a refill?"

2. (If refill) "Did you call it in or drop off the request?"

3. "What is the medication, and who prescribed it for you?"

C. Empathize; validate the patient/customer's perspective
"It can be frustrating to wait for something like that."

II. Acknowledge

A. Apologize—without assigning blame or guilt
"I'm sorry we've delayed you."

B. Explain what you can do; provide general overview of the process you will follow to resolve the concern
"I'll call the pharmacy and find out when your prescription should be ready" (may require additional call to MD's office to determine when authorization will occur).

   C. Agree on next contact

      "This may take me a few minutes. Would you like to have a cup of coffee on us while you're waiting? Here's a voucher you can use at the Volunteer table."

III. Problem Solve

   A. Consult with others

      1. Exchange information

      2. Identify options

   B. Update patient/customer if necessary

      1. "The pharmacy was waiting for the authorization from your physician. Apparently you recently had some tests done, and he wanted to check the results to see if he needed to change the dosage."

      2. "Our pharmacy is open until _____ this evening. Would you like to come back later, or would it be more convenient for you to pick up this prescription at another Plan facility?"

IV. Follow-Up

   A. Bring closure to complaint

      Summarize patient/customer's request, the actions you took, and agreed-upon resolution

   B. Thank patient/customer

      "I appreciate your telling me about this. I know it's frustrating to have to wait. Our intent is to make sure you're getting the right medication and the right amount."

   C. Offer to assist in the future if needed

      1. "In case you have any questions later, here's my name and the clinic phone number."

      2. "We have a phone number you can use 24 hours a day to call in your request for a refill. Let me give that to you so you'll have it in the future."

   D. Document complaint and distribute, if appropriate

▼ Medical Receptionist

Quality of Care

I. Patient/Customer Contact

   A. Listen—focus on the patient/customer with attentive body language (if in person) and voice inflections (if over the telephone)

   B. Empathize; validate the patient/customer's perspective

      1. "It must be frustrating to feel that you're not getting better."

2. "It sounds like this has been a difficult time for you."

II. Acknowledge

A. Apologize—without assigning blame or guilt

1. "I'm sorry you're unhappy with your care."

2. "I'm sorry you're still having health problems."

B. Explain what you can do; provide general overview of the process you will follow to resolve the concern

1. "Would you like me to schedule an appointment for you with Dr. _____ so you can discuss these concerns with him [her]? I know he [she] wants you to be satisfied with your care."

2. "I will document your concern and share it with the chief of staff for our clinic. I can also transfer you to our physician selection person to help you choose a different physician."

C. Agree on next contact
(If referred to chief of staff) "Would you like someone to call you back on this? [name] is our Patient Representative, and is the best person to follow up with you on this."

III. Problem Solve

A. Consult with others—refer to chief of staff or to Patient Representative for follow-up Exchange information

B. Update patient/customer if necessary

IV. Follow-Up

A. Bring closure to complaint

summarize patient/customer's request, the actions you took, and agreed-upon resolution

B. Thank patient/customer
"Thank you for sharing your concerns with me. We want you to have confidence in the care you receive here."

C. Share your organization's Service Recovery standards, if appropriate

1. You strive to recognize the patient/customer as an individual

2. You strive to provide the patient/customer with an easy, obvious process for sharing concerns

3. You strive to provide the patient/customer with a key contact person

4. You strive for a fair resolution

5. You strive for a fast resolution

6. You strive to provide consistent, clear, and accurate information

D. Written follow-up letter

1. Summarize patient/customer's request, the actions you took, and agreed-upon resolution

2. Apologize for the patient/customer's feelings of dissatisfaction or inconvenience

3. Report any system changes that have occurred as a result of this complaint

4. Offer to assist in the future if needed

E. Document complaint and distribute, if appropriate

▼ Medical Receptionist

Timely Return Call from Registered Nurse

I. Patient/Customer Contact

A. Listen—focus on the patient/customer with attentive body language (if in person) and voice inflections (if over the telephone)

B. Ask open-ended questions

1. "What time did you call?"

2. "How long have you waited?"

C. Empathize; validate the patient/customer's perspective
"It can be frustrating to wait for a call-back when you're sick [you have a sick child]."

II. Acknowledge

A. Apologize—without assigning blame or guilt
"I'm sorry you've had trouble getting through to the nurse."

B. Explain what you can do; provide general overview of the process you will follow to resolve the concern
"Let me check and see if she can talk to you now. Would you mind holding for a minute?"

C. Agree on next contact
"She will be able to call you back between ___:___ and ___:___ . Will you still be at this number?"

III. Follow-Up

A. Bring closure to complaint
Summarize patient/customer's request, the actions you took, and agreed-upon resolution

B. Thank patient/customer
"I appreciate your telling me about the problem you've had getting through this morning."

C. Share your organization's Service Recovery standards, if appropriate

1. You strive to recognize the patient/customer as an individual
2. You strive to provide the patient/customer with an easy, obvious process for sharing concerns
3. You strive to provide the patient/customer with a key contact person
4. You strive for a fair resolution
5. You strive for a fast resolution
6. You strive to provide consistent, clear, and accurate information

D. Document complaint and distribute, if appropriate

▼ Medical Receptionist

Telephone Access

I. Patient/Customer Contact

   A. Listen—focus on the patient/customer with attentive body language (if in person) and voice inflections (if over the telephone)

   B. Ask open-ended questions
   1. "What time did you call?"
   2. "How long did you have to wait?"

   C. Empathize; validate the patient/customer's perspective
   "It can be frustrating to not get through on the telephone."

II. Acknowledge

   A. Apologize—without assigning blame or guilt
   "I'm sorry you had trouble getting through."

   B. Explain what you can do; provide general overview of the process you will follow to resolve the concern
   1. "I can take a message for you and have _____ call you back."
   2. "I'll also document your complaint and refer it to our Patient Representative. She is reviewing telephone access problems right now."
   3. "Our least busy telephone times are from 10:30 to 12:30 in the morning and after 3:00 in the afternoon."

   C. Agree on next contact
   "Would you like her to call you back about this?"

III. Follow-Up

   A. Bring closure to complaint
   Summarize patient/customer's request, the actions you took, and agreed-upon resolution

B. Thank patient/customer
"I appreciate your telling me about the problem you had getting through this morning."

C. Share your organization's Service Recovery standards, if appropriate

　1. You strive to recognize the patient/customer as an individual

　2. You strive to provide the patient/customer with an easy, obvious process for sharing concerns

　3. You strive to provide the patient/customer with a key contact person

　4. You strive for a fair resolution

　5. You strive for a fast resolution

　6. You strive to provide consistent, clear, and accurate information

D. Document complaint and distribute, if appropriate

▼ Medical Receptionist

Waiting Room Delay

Note: The best way to avoid this complaint is to anticipate the problem and give patient/customers the option of waiting or rescheduling before they begin to complain.

I. Patient/Customer Contact

A. Listen—focus on the patient/customer with attentive body language (if in person) and voice inflections (if over the telephone)

B. Ask open-ended questions
"What time was your appointment supposed to be?"

C. Empathize; validate the patient/customer's perspective
"It can be frustrating to wait for something like that."

II. Acknowledge

A. Apologize—without assigning blame or guilt
"I'm sorry we've delayed you."

B. Explain what you can do; provide general overview of the process you will follow to resolve the concern

　1. "The Doctor was delayed by an emergency." [**OR** "The Doctor had to admit a patient to the hospital," **OR** "The Doctor had a seriously ill patient who had to be seen immediately.]"

　2. "It will probably be at least another half hour before he can see you. Would you like to stay, or would you prefer to reschedule for another day?"

III. Follow-Up

    A. Bring closure to complaint
Summarize patient/customer's request, the actions you took, and agreed-upon resolution
Note: Make every effort to reschedule the patient for the earliest date possible—don't add insult to injury.

    B. Thank patient/customer
"I appreciate your telling me about this. I know it's frustrating to have to wait. We try to stay on schedule, but we can't always predict emergencies."

    C. Share your organization's Service Recovery standards, if appropriate

        1. You strive to recognize the patient/customer as an individual

        2. You strive to provide the patient/customer with an easy, obvious process for sharing concerns

        3. You strive to provide the patient/customer with a key contact person

        4. You strive for a fair resolution

        5. You strive for a fast resolution

        6. You strive to provide consistent, clear, and accurate information

    D. Offer to assist in the future if needed
"In case you have any questions later, here's my name and the clinic phone number."

    E. Document complaint and distribute, if appropriate

Appendix B

Service Recovery Protocols for Physicians

Service Recovery, as described in Chapter 2, involves five basic steps. Below is a model for developing Service Recovery protocols for complaints heard by physicians, followed by some ideas for how these encounters might be handled.

Model

I. Patient/Customer Contact

    A. Listen—focus on the patient/customer with attentive body language (if in person) and voice inflections (if over the telephone)

    B. Ask open-ended questions

    C. Empathize; validate the patient/customer's perspective

    D. Clarify the patient/customer's expectation for resolution

II. Acknowledge

    A. Apologize—without assigning blame or guilt

    B. Verify the facts

    C. Explain what you can do; provide general overview of the process you will follow to resolve the concern

    D. Agree on next contact
       "I'm going to look into this for you and get back to you [time frame]"—hopefully in 24 hours/up to 48 hours.

III. Problem Solve
   A. Consult with others
      1. Exchange information
      2. Collect information for explaining resolution
      3. Identify options
      4. Together, ask what's the right thing to do; what can we do; what will we do
   B. Explore options
      1. Identify options
      2. Together, ask what's the right thing to do; what can we do; what will we do
   C. Update patient/customer if necessary

IV. Respond/Refer
   A. Contact patient/customer with customized resolution
   B. Transfer complaint, if appropriate, to another department/division/region etc.
      1. Contact the resource person and relay all the pertinent information and facts about the problem
      2. Negotiate with the resource person to assume responsibility for investigating, reviewing, and/or resolving the problem; determine who will notify the patient/customer with the final resolution
      3. Advise the patient/customer of the next step, including who the resource person is and how to reach him or her
      4. Document in writing the pertinent facts and the plan for resolution, and send a copy to the resource person
   C. Update patient/customer if necessary

V. Follow-Up
   A. Bring closure to complaint
       Summarize patient/customer's request, the actions you took, and agreed-upon resolution.
   B. Thank patient/customer
   C. Share your organization's Service Recovery standards, if appropriate
      1. You strive to recognize the patient/customer as an individual
      2. You strive to provide the patient/customer with an easy, obvious process for sharing concerns
      3. You strive to provide the patient/customer with a key contact person
      4. You strive for a fair resolution
      5. You strive for a fast resolution
      6. You strive to provide consistent, clear, and accurate information

D. Written follow-up letter

1. Summarize patient/customer's request, the actions you took, and agreed-upon resolution

2. Apologize for the patient/customer's feelings of dissatisfaction or inconvenience

3. Report any system changes that have occurred as a result of this complaint

4. Offer to assist in the future if needed

E. Document complaint and distribute, if appropriate

Service Recovery Standards

85% of all complaints are resolved by the person who hears the complaint

85% of all complaints are resolved the same day

Complex complaints are resolved within two weeks

▼ Physicians

Waiting Room Delay

Note: If the physician enters the exam room more than 15 minutes after the scheduled time of the appointment, it is appropriate to apologize immediately. If this is the first appointment with the patient, the physician should introduce herself, spend a couple of minutes on Service Recovery, and then move on to discuss the patient's medical problem.

I. Patient/Customer Contact
Listen—focus on the patient/customer with attentive body language. If this is the first appointment, come into the room, shake the patient's hand, and introduce yourself.

II. Acknowledge

A. Apologize—without assigning blame or guilt

1. "I'm sorry you had to wait."

2. "I'm sorry I was delayed. I hope this hasn't upset your schedule for today."

B. Verify the facts

1. "The patient scheduled just before you turned out to have a more serious problem than we expected, and I had to make arrangements to admit him to the hospital."

2. "We had several emergency cases this morning, which has thrown our whole schedule off."

C. Explain what you can do; provide general overview of the process you will follow to resolve the concern

1. "Do you have time to stay for the appointment, or do you need to reschedule?"
2. "I can ask [receptionist] to schedule you for the next available appointment."

III. Follow-Up

A. Thank patient/customer

1. "I appreciate your understanding and patience today."
2. "Thank you for being so understanding."

▼ Physicians
Quality of Care

I. Patient/Customer Contact

A. Listen—focus on the patient/customer with attentive body language (if in person) and voice inflections (if over the telephone)

B. Ask open-ended questions

1. "I understand you have some concerns about your diagnosis [treatment plan]. Can you tell me what those concerns are?"
2. "I want you to feel comfortable with the treatment plan. What questions do you have?"

C. Empathize; validate the patient/customer's perspective

1. "This has not been an easy time for you."
2. "I understand how frustrating this has been for you."

D. Clarify the patient/customer's expectation for resolution

II. Acknowledge

A. Apologize—without assigning blame or guilt
"I'm sorry this illness has been so difficult [frustrating] for you and your family."

B. Verify the facts
Summarize the symptoms, test results, and what led to the diagnosis [treatment plan]

C. Explain what you can do; provide general overview of the process you will follow to resolve the concern
"If you are not comfortable with my suggestions, I can review your records with Dr. _____, chief of _____, or my receptionist can schedule you for a second opinion appointment with Dr. _____."

D. Agree on next contact
"I'm going to review your case with Dr. _____, and get back to you [time frame]" —hopefully in 24 hours/up to 48 hours

III. Problem Solve

   A. Consult with others

      1. Exchange information

      2. Collect information for explaining resolution

      3. Identify options

   B. Update patient/customer, if necessary

IV. Respond/Refer

   A. Contact patient/customer with customized resolution

   B. Transfer complaint, if appropriate, to another department/division/region etc.

      1. Contact the resource person, and relay all the pertinent information and facts about the problem

      2. Negotiate with the resource person to assume responsibility for investigating, reviewing, and/or resolving the problem; determine who will notify the patient/customer with the final resolution

      3. Advise the patient/customer of the next step, including who the resource person is and how to reach him or her

      4. Document in writing the pertinent facts and the plan for resolution, and send a copy to the resource person

   C. Update patient/customer if necessary

V. Follow-Up

   A. Bring closure to complaint
      Summarize patient/customer's request, the actions you took, and agreed-upon resolution

   B. Thank patient/customer
      "I appreciate your telling me about your concerns. I want you to have confidence in the care and service you receive from our office."

▼ Physicians

Appointment with Mid-Level Practitioner

I. Patient/Customer Contact

   A. Listen—focus on the patient/customer with attentive body language (if in person) and voice inflections (if over the telephone)

   B. Ask open-ended questions
      "I understand that you were uncomfortable being seen by our physician assistant [nurse practitioner], even though they could have seen you earlier. Can you tell me why you were concerned?"

    C. Empathize; validate the patient/customer's perspective
       "I can certainly understand your wish to receive the best possible medical care."

    D. Clarify the patient/customer's expectation for resolution
       "As I understand it, you want to be sure your care is the best possible."

II. Acknowledge

    A. Apologize—without assigning blame or guilt
       "I'm sorry you felt you were being offered low quality care."

    B. Verify the facts
       "Let me tell you about our physician assistant's [nurse practitioner's] qualifications and their role in our healthcare team."

    C. Explain what you can do; provide general overview of the process you will follow to resolve the concern
       "If you prefer to only see a physician, we can certainly accommodate that. However, you may not be scheduled as quickly for some of these routine problems."

III. Follow-Up

    A. Bring closure to complaint
       Summarize patient/customer's request, the actions you took, and agreed-upon resolution

    B. Thank patient/customer
       "I'm glad you shared your concerns with me, and I hope the information I gave you is helpful. We want you to have confidence in the medical care and services we provide you and your family."

▼ Physicians

Noncovered Service

I. Patient/Customer Contact

    A. Listen—focus on the patient/customer with attentive body language (if in person) and voice inflections (if over the telephone)

    B. Ask open-ended questions

    C. Empathize; validate the patient/customer's perspective

    D. Clarify the patient/customer's expectation for resolution

II. Acknowledge

    A. Apologize—without assigning blame or guilt

    B. Verify the facts

C. Explain what you can do; provide general overview of the process you will follow to resolve the concern

D. Agree on next contact
"I'm going to look into this for you and get back to you [time frame]" —hopefully in 24 hours/up to 48 hours

III. Problem Solve

A. Consult with others

1. Exchange information

2. Collect information for explaining resolution

3. Identify options

4. Together, ask what's the right thing to do; what can we do; what will we do

B. Explore options

1. Identify options

2. Together, ask what's the right thing to do; what can we do; what will we do

C. Update patient/customer if necessary

IV. Respond/Refer

A. Contact patient/customer with customized resolution

B. Transfer complaint, if appropriate, to another department/division/region etc.

1. Contact the resource person, and relay all the pertinent information and facts about the problem

2. Negotiate with the resource person to assume responsibility for investigating, reviewing, and/or resolving the problem; determine who will notify the patient/customer with the final resolution

3. Advise the patient/customer of the next step, including who the resource person is and how to reach him or her

4. Document in writing the pertinent facts and the plan for resolution, and send a copy to the resource person

C. Update patient/customer if necessary

V. Follow-Up

A. Bring closure to complaint
Summarize patient/customer's request, the actions you took, and agreed-upon resolution

B. Thank patient/customer

C. Share your organization's Service Recovery standards, if appropriate

1. You strive to recognize the patient/customer as an individual

2. You strive to provide the patient/customer with an easy, obvious process for sharing concerns

3. You strive to provide the patient/customer with a key contact person

4. You strive for a fair resolution

5. You strive for a fast resolution

6. You strive to provide consistent, clear, and accurate information

D. Written follow-up letter

1. Summarize patient/customer's request, the actions you took, and agreed-upon resolution

2. Apologize for the patient/customer's feelings of dissatisfaction or inconvenience

3. Report any system changes that have occurred as a result of this complaint

4. Offer to assist in the future if needed

E. Document complaint and distribute, if appropriate

Service Recovery Standards

85% of all complaints are resolved by the person who hears the complaint

85% of all complaints are resolved the same day

Complex complaints are resolved within two weeks

Appendix C

Service Recovery Protocols for the Patient Representative Department

Service Recovery, as described in Chapter 2, involves five basic steps. Below is a model for developing Service Recovery protocols for a centralized patient representative department at an administrative level, followed by some ideas for how these calls might be handled.

Model

I. Patient/Customer Contact

    A. Listen—focus on the patient/customer with attentive body language (if in person) and voice inflections (if over the telephone)

    B. Ask open-ended questions

    C. Empathize; validate the patient/customer's perspective

    D. Clarify the patient/customer's expectation for resolution

II. Acknowledge

    A. Apologize—without assigning blame or guilt

    B. Verify the facts

149

Appendix C

    C. Explain what you can do; provide general overview of the process you will follow to resolve the concern

    D. Agree on next contact
"I'm going to look into this for you and get back to you [time frame]"—hopefully in 24 hours/up to 48 hours

III. Problem Solve

    A. Consult with others

       1. Exchange information

       2. Collect information for explaining resolution

       3. Identify options

       4. Together, ask what's the right thing to do; what can we do; what will we do

    B. Explore options

       1. Identify options

       2. Together, ask what's the right thing to do; what can we do; what will we do

    C. Update consumer if necessary

IV. Respond/Refer

    A. Contact patient/customer with customized resolution

    B. Transfer complaint, if appropriate, to another department/division/region etc.

       1. Contact the resource person and relay all the pertinent information and facts about the problem

       2. Negotiate with the resource person to assume responsibility for investigating, reviewing, and/or resolving the problem; determine who will notify the patient/customer with the final resolution

       3. Advise the patient/customer of the next step, including who the resource person is and how to reach him or her

       4. Document in writing the pertinent facts and the plan for resolution, and send a copy to the resource person

    C. Update patient/customer if necessary

V. Follow-Up

    A. Bring closure to complaint
Summarize patient/customer's request, the actions you took, and agreed-upon resolution

    B. Thank patient/customer

    C. Share your organization's Service Recovery standards, if appropriate

       1. You strive to recognize the patient/customer as an individual

       2. You strive to provide the patient/customer with an easy, obvious process for sharing concerns

3. You strive to provide the patient/customer with a key contact person

4. You strive for a fair resolution

5. You strive for a fast resolution

6. You strive to provide consistent, clear, and accurate information

D. Written follow-up letter

1. Summarize patient/customer's request, the actions you took, and agreed-upon resolution

2. Apologize for the patient/customer's feelings of dissatisfaction or inconvenience

3. Report any system changes that have occurred as a result of this complaint

4. Offer to assist in the future if needed

E. Document complaint and distribute, if appropriate

Service Recovery Standards

85% of all complaints are resolved by the person who hears the complaint

85% of all complaints are resolved the same day

Complex complaints are resolved within two weeks

▼ Patient Representative Department

Appointment Wait Time

I. Patient/Customer Contact

A. Listen—focus on the patient/customer with attentive body language (if in person) and voice inflections (if over the telephone)

B. Ask open-ended questions

1. "Who have you talked to about this [and when]?"

2. "What are your symptoms?" ["Are these new or more severe since you were referred?"]

3. "Who is your primary care physician?"

4. "What else has your physician recommended to treat this problem?"

5. "What is your concern about waiting until _____?" (ask only if it's not clear why person can't wait—do not antagonize person further).

6. "Is there anything else I need to be aware of?"

C. Empathize; validate the patient/customer's perspective

1. "I'm sure you must be . . ."

2. "I understand this is very frustrating for you."

3. "It sounds like you're . . ."

4. "I'm glad you let me know that . . ."

D. Clarify expectation for resolution

1. "When did you want to be seen?"

2. "When are you available—are there any times you cannot come for an appointment?"

3. "Would you be willing to go to another Plan facility in _____ or _____ ?"

II. Acknowledge

A. Apologize—without assigning blame or guilt

1. "I'm sorry this isn't convenient."

2. "I'm sorry this isn't what you were expecting."

B. Verify the facts
"Let me make sure I understand what you've told me. . ."

C. Explain what you can do; provide general overview of the process you will follow to resolve the concern

D. Agree on next contact
"I'm going to look into this for you and get back to you [time frame]"—hopefully in 24 hours/up to 48 hours

III. Problem Solve

A. Consult with others

1. If primary care appointment access, call the primary care team—RN or MD

2. If specialty care appointment access, and patient accepts referral urgency level

a. Call specialty services "head nurse" or nurse manager

b. Call section chief or facility manager

c. Call another facility

d. Call referral services department for outside referral

3. If specialty care appointment access, and patient disagrees with referral urgency level

a. Call referring physician

b. Offer second primary care opinion

4. Collect information for explaining resolution

5. Identify options

6. Together, ask what's the right thing to do; what can we do; what will we do

C. Update patient/customer if necessary

IV. Respond/Refer

    A. Contact patient/customer with customized resolution

    B. Based on patient's temperament, provide explanation of why the Plan schedules appointments the way it does

        1. Verify that appointment scheduling is driven by the triage process

        2. If waiting would adversely affect patient's condition, he or she would be seen earlier

    C. Transfer complaint, if appropriate, to another department/division/region etc.

        1. Contact the resource person, and relay all the pertinent information and facts about the problem

        2. Negotiate with the resource person to assume responsibility for investigating, reviewing, and/or resolving the problem; determine who will notify the patient/customer with the final resolution

        3. Advise the patient/customer of the next step, including who the resource person is and how to reach him or her

        4. Document in writing the pertinent facts and the plan for resolution, and send a copy to the resource person

    D. Update patient/customer if necessary

V. Follow-Up

    A. Bring closure to complaint
Summarize patient/customer's request, the actions you took, and agreed-upon resolution

    B. Thank patient/customer

    C. Share your organization's Service Recovery standards, if appropriate

        1. You strive to recognize the patient/customer as an individual

        2. You strive to provide the patient/customer with an easy, obvious process for sharing concerns

        3. You strive to provide the patient/customer with a key contact person

        4. You strive for a fair resolution

        5. You strive for a fast resolution

        6. You strive to provide consistent, clear, and accurate information

    D. Written follow-up letter

        1. Summarize patient/customer's request, the actions you took, and agreed-upon resolution

2. Apologize for the patient/customer's feelings of dissatisfaction or inconvenience

3. Report any system changes that have occurred as a result of this complaint

4. Offer to assist in the future if needed

E. Document complaint and distribute, if appropriate

▼ Patient Representative Department
Staff Attitude or Customer-Service Orientation

I. Patient/Customer Contact

A. Listen—focus on the patient/customer with attentive body language (if in person) and voice inflections (if over the telephone)

B. Ask open-ended questions

1. "Who said this to you? When?"

2. "What specifically did he [she] say?"

3. "Can you describe the situation in more detail for me?"

C. Empathize; validate the patient/customer's perspective
"It sounds like that was a difficult [awkward/ frustrating] situation for you."

II. Acknowledge

A. Apologize—without assigning blame or guilt

1. "I'm sorry you felt _____."

2. "I'm sure it wasn't their intent to _____."

B. Verify the facts

C. Explain what you can do; provide general overview of the process you will follow to resolve the concern

"I will be documenting your complaint and . . ."

a. [If physician] ". . . sending a copy to his [her] section/clinic chief. This will also be included in the information we provide for the physicians' annual evaluations."

b. [If other employee] ". . . sending a copy to his [her] supervisor for follow-up with him [her]."

D. Clarify expectation for resolution

"Is there anything else you would like done?"

a. Change primary care physician—transfer patient to Physician Selection

b. Second opinion appointment—transfer to the appropriate section/cluster for appointment scheduling

      c. Refund of co-pay—follow guidelines developed by administration for do-
         ing this efficiently

      d. Payment of outside bill—request copy of bills (itemized with procedure
         codes) and outside records

  E. Agree on next contact

    1. "I'm going to look into this for you and get back to you [time frame]"—
       hopefully in 24 hours/up to 48 hours

    2. "I'm going to transfer you to Physician Selection [the _____ department/
       office] to change physicians [schedule an appointment]."

    3. "I will send you a medical records release form that you can sign and give
       to the community physician. His office will then send the records directly
       to me."

    4. "I will review this with the chief of staff [the clinic/the section], and get
       back to you [time frame]"—hopefully in 24 hours/up to 48 hours

III. Problem Solve

  A. Consult with others

    1. Exchange information

    2. Collect information for explaining resolution

    3. Identify options

    4. Together, ask what's the right thing to do; what can we do; what will we do

  B. Explore options

    1. Identify options

    2. Together, ask what's the right thing to do; what can we do; what will we do

  C. Update patient/customer if necessary

IV. Respond/Refer

  A. Contact patient/customer with customized resolution

  B. Educate staff—if patient was obnoxious, it is not okay for staff to retaliate; we
    have a responsibility to maintain professionalism

  C. Transfer complaint, if appropriate, to another department/division/region etc.

    1. Contact the resource person and relay all the pertinent information and facts
       about the problem

    2. Negotiate with the resource person to assume responsibility for investigating,
       reviewing, and/or resolving the problem; determine who will notify the pa-
       tient/customer with the final resolution

    3. Advise the patient/customer of the next step, including who the resource per-
       son is and how to reach him or her

4. Document in writing the pertinent facts and the plan for resolution, and send a copy to the resource person

D. Update patient/customer if necessary

V. Follow-Up

A. Bring closure to complaint
Summarize patient/customer's request, the actions you took, and agreed-upon resolution

B. Thank patient/customer

C. Share your organization's Service Recovery standards, if appropriate

1. You strive to recognize the patient/customer as an individual

2. You strive to provide the patient/customer with an easy, obvious process for sharing concerns

3. You strive to provide the patient/customer with a key contact person

4. You strive for a fair resolution

5. You strive for a fast resolution

6. You strive to provide consistent, clear, and accurate information

D. Written follow-up letter

1. Summarize patient/customer's request, the actions you took, and agreed-upon resolution

2. Apologize for the patient/customer's feelings of dissatisfaction or inconvenience

3. Report any system changes that have occurred as a result of this complaint

4. Offer to assist in the future if needed

E. Document complaint and distribute, as appropriate

▼ Patient Representative Department
Handling of Complaints and Concerns

I. Patient/Customer Contact

A. Listen—focus on the patient/customer with attentive body language (if in person) and voice inflections (if over the telephone)

B. Ask open-ended questions
"What part of the complaint handling didn't you like?"

C. Empathize; validate the patient/customer's perspective
"I understand that this has been inconvenient for you."

D. Clarify expectations for resolution

1. "What would you like to see happen?"

2. "Why do you think it should happen this way?"

3. "What do you think would be a fair resolution?"

4. "How soon do you need a response from us?"

5. "Why do you need an immediate response?"

II. Acknowledge

    A. Verify facts
"Let me summarize what you've told me to be sure I have all the information."

    B. Apologize—without assigning blame or guilt
"I'm sorry we haven't been able to meet your needs; it certainly is not our intent."

    C. Explain what you can do; provide general overview of the process you will follow to resolve the concern
"I will contact the manager of that department to see if there is something we can do to make this right for you."

    D. Agree on next contact
"I'm going to look into this for you and get back to you [time frame]—hopefully in 24 hours/up to 48 hours

III. Problem Solve

    A. Consult with others

        1. If access or quality-of-care issue, consult with primary-care team

        2. If coverage is at issue, consult with Contract Administration or Medical Coverage Department

        3. If it isn't clear who can help, consult with next level of administration or Patient Representative manager

    B. Explore options

        1. Consider possible exceptions

        2. Together, ask what's the right thing to do; what can we do; what will we do

        3. Explore if further review or appeal is available (consult with next level of administration or Patient Representative manager)

    C. Update patient/customer if necessary

IV. Respond/Refer

    A. Contact patient/customer with customized resolution

    B. Transfer complaint, if appropriate, to next level of administration or Patient Representative manager

        1. Contact the resource person and relay all the pertinent information and facts about the problem

        2. Negotiate with the resource person to assume responsibility for investigating, reviewing, and/or resolving the problem; determine who will notify the patient/customer with the final resolution

   3. Advise the patient/customer of the next step, including who the resource person is and how to reach him or her

   4. Document in writing the pertinent facts and the plan for resolution, and send a copy to the resource person

 C. Update patient/customer if necessary

V. Follow-Up

 A. Bring closure to complaint
    Summarize patient/customer's request, the actions you took, and agreed-upon resolution

 B. Thank patient/customer

 C. Share your organization's Service Recovery standards, if appropriate

   1. You strive to recognize the patient/customer as an individual

   2. You strive to provide the patient/customer with an easy, obvious process for sharing concerns

   3. You strive to provide the patient/customer with a key contact person

   4. You strive for a fair resolution

   5. You strive for a fast resolution

   6. You strive to provide consistent, clear, and accurate information

 D. Written follow-up letter

   1. Summarize patient/customer's request, the actions you took, and agreed-upon resolution

   2. Apologize for the patient/customer's feelings of dissatisfaction or inconvenience

   3. Report any system changes that have occurred as a result of this complaint

   4. Offer to assist in the future if needed

 E. Document complaint and distribute, if appropriate

▼ Patient Representative Department

Not Active on System/New Enrollee, Denied Services

I. Patient/Customer Contact

 A. Listen—focus on the patient/customer with attentive body language (if in person) and voice inflections (if over the telephone)

 B. Empathize; validate the patient/customer's perspective
    "I can understand your frustration."

 C. Ask open-ended questions

   1. "Where were you denied services?"

      2. "Who is your employer?"

      3. "Do you know when your coverage began?"

      4. "Did you fill out an enrollment card [form]?"

      5. "May I have your middle initial and the spelling of your last name?"

  D. Clarify expectation for resolution

      1. "How can we make this right for you?"

      2. "How can I help you?"

II. Acknowledge

  A. Apologize—without assigning blame or guilt

      1. "I'm sorry your first contact with us was so disappointing/upsetting/etc."

      2. "I'm sorry you've had difficulty."

  B. Verify the facts
    "Let me see if I understand what happened . . ."

  C. Explain what you can do; provide general overview of the process you will follow to resolve the concern

      1. "I am going to contact the Member Services Department in our insurance division to research the status of your enrollment, and I will contact the Physician Selection person at the clinic to assist you in scheduling an appointment. Their phone numbers are: ____–_____ and ____–_____ . If you have not heard back from them by [up to 48 hours, depending on the urgency of need for care], please call me back. My name is _____ , and the telephone number here is ____–_____ ."

      2. "It sounds like you need to be seen right away. We can go ahead and arrange an appointment for you, with the understanding that if your coverage is not yet in effect you will be responsible for the bill."

      3. "Let me help you with this. Usually we prefer to go ahead and schedule services for customers even if they have not received their ID cards. I'll verify your coverage and call you with your consumer number."

  D. Agree on next contact
    "I'm going to look into this for you and get back to you (time frame)"—hopefully in 24 hours/up to 48 hours

III. Problem Solve

  A. Consult with others—Member Services Information Line

      1. Information exchange—may not have ID number [card] because

        a. Not eligible due to

          • Employer's probationary period

- Have other carrier coverage through employer
- Coverage not effective yet

    b. Eligible but enrollment form not yet received

2. Collect information for explaining resolution

3. Identify options

4. Together, ask what's the right thing to do; what can we do; what will we do

B. Explore options

    1. Identify options

        a. Agree to see patient although coverage not yet effective with understanding that we will bill for the services

        b. Assist with seeking care in the community

    2. Together, ask what's the right thing to do; what can we do; what will we do

C. Update patient/customer if necessary

IV. Respond/Refer

    A. Contact patient/customer with customized resolution

        1. "Your patient number is _____, and I can transfer you to your medical center's Physician Selection person to choose a physician and to schedule an appointment; or I can give you the number for you to call at your convenience."

        2. "You will be receiving your ID card within _____ days. If you do not receive it, please call me back. My name is _____, and my number is ____–_____."

        3. "When I was researching your concern, I found that you are not covered by this Plan. I suggest you contact your personnel department to look into it for you."

        4. "Because you need medical care, my suggestion is that you contact the community Physician Referral service. They have information about community physicians such as if they are Board certified and if they accept your insurance."

    B. Transfer complaint, if appropriate, to another department/division/region etc.

        1. Contact the resource person and relay all the pertinent information and facts about the problem

        2. Negotiate with the resource person to assume responsibility for investigating, reviewing, and/or resolving the problem; determine who will notify the patient/customer with the final resolution

        3. Advise the patient/customer of the next step, including who the resource person is and how to reach him or her

4. Document in writing the pertinent facts and the plan for resolution, and send a copy to the resource person

C. Update patient/customer if necessary

V. Follow-Up

A. Bring closure to complaint
Summarize patient/customer's request, the actions you took, and agreed-upon resolution

B. Thank patient/customer

1. "Thank you for calling us, and I'm sorry this was confusing to sort out. I appreciate your patience while we researched your coverage status."

2. "Thank you for calling us, and I'm sorry we weren't able to see you. I hope that if you have the opportunity to choose our Plan in the future, you will consider joining us."

C. Share your organization's Service Recovery standards, if appropriate

1. You strive to recognize the patient/customer as an individual

2. You strive to provide the patient/customer with an easy, obvious process for sharing concerns

3. You strive to provide the patient/customer with a key contact person

4. You strive for a fair resolution

5. You strive for a fast resolution

6. You strive to provide consistent, clear, and accurate information

D. Written follow-up letter

1. Summarize patient/customer's request, the actions you took, and agreed-upon resolution

2. Apologize for the patient/customer's feelings of dissatisfaction or inconvenience

3. Report any system changes that have occurred as a result of this complaint

4. Offer to assist in the future if needed

E. Document complaint and distribute, if appropriate

▼ Patient Representative Department

Mid-Level Practitioner Appointment, Not MD Appointment

I. Patient/Customer Contact

A. Listen—focus on the patient/customer with attentive body language (if in person) and voice inflections (if over the telephone)

B. Ask open-ended questions

1. "Would you tell me what happened?" (including why appointment is needed)
2. "Were you offered an appointment with an MD?"
3. "Was it your understanding that the appointment was with an MD?"
4. "Could you tell me your concerns about seeing a physician assistant [nurse practitioner]?"

C. Empathize; validate the patient/customer's perspective

1. "It sounds like you would prefer to see an MD rather than a physician assistant [nurse practitioner]."
2. "It sounds like you were not satisfied with your appointment with the physician assistant [nurse practitioner]."

D. Clarify expectation for resolution
"What do you think would be a fair resolution?"

II. Acknowledge

A. Apologize—without assigning blame or guilt

1. "I'm sorry you can't [didn't] see the provider you expected to see."
2. "I'm sorry a physician appointment wasn't [isn't] available at a time that was [is] convenient for you."

B. Verify the facts

III. Problem Solve

A. Explore options

1. "I'd be happy to assist you in scheduling an appointment with a physician."
2. "When did you want to be seen?"
3. "When are you available—are there any times you cannot come for an appointment?"
4. "Would you be willing to go to another Plan facility in _____ or _____?"

C. Provide information and explain—background and training of physician assistants [nurse practitioners], how they are used, etc.

D. Verify that patient/customer still insists on seeing MD, even after explanation of PA/NP's scope of practice

IV. Respond/Refer

A. Contact patient/customer with customized resolution
"I have contacted Dr. _____'s office, and you have an appointment at _____ on _____."

B. Transfer consumer to MD's office for assistance with scheduling **after** advising consumer to call you back if any further difficulties.

1. Contact the resource person, and relay all the pertinent information and facts about the problem

2. Negotiate with the resource person to assume responsibility for investigating, reviewing, and/or resolving the problem; determine who will notify the patient/customer with the final resolution

3. Advise the patient/customer of the next step, including who the resource person is and how to reach him or her

4. Document in writing the pertinent facts and the plan for resolution, and send a copy to the resource person

V. Follow-Up

   A. Bring closure to complaint
Summarize patient/customer's request, the actions you took, and agreed-upon resolution

   B. Thank patient/customer

   C. Share your organization's Service Recovery standards, if appropriate

     1. You strive to recognize the patient/customer as an individual

     2. You strive to provide the patient/customer with an easy, obvious process for sharing concerns

     3. You strive to provide the patient/customer with a key contact person

     4. You strive for a fair resolution

     5. You strive for a fast resolution

     6. You strive to provide consistent, clear, and accurate information

   D. Written follow-up letter

     1. Summarize patient/customer's request, the actions you took, and agreed-upon resolution

     2. Apologize for the patient/customer's feelings of dissatisfaction or inconvenience

     3. Report any system changes that have occurred as a result of this complaint

     4. Offer to assist in the future if needed

   E. Document complaint and distribute, if appropriate

▼ Patient Representative Department

Quality of Care

Note: For more serious or complex quality-of-care concerns, refer to Chapter 4.

I. Patient/Customer Contact

   A. Listen—focus on the patient/customer with attentive body language (if in person) and voice inflections (if over the telephone)

   B. Ask open-ended questions

     1. "Who was the physician?"

2. "When did this happen?"

3. "Can you describe the situation in more detail for me?"

C. Empathize; validate the patient/customer's perspective

1. "It must be frustrating to feel that you're not getting better."

2. "I understand what you are saying; cancer is a frightening diagnosis."

3. "I hear the pain [frustration] in your voice."

4. "It sounds like this has been a difficult time for you."

II. Acknowledge

A. Apologize—without assigning blame or guilt

1. "I'm sorry you're unhappy with your care."

2. "I'm sorry you've lost confidence in your doctor."

3. "I'm sorry you're still having health problems."

B. Verify the facts

1. "Who is the complaint about? [an individual provider, an office, or a system (e.g., cancer screening)]."

2. "When and where did the problem occur?"

3. Review/summarize back the complaint; paraphrase—make sure you understand the sequence of events, and what the consumer believes are cause-and-effect relationships.

C. Clarify expectation for resolution

1. "We usually document complaints such as this and..."

   a. [if physician] "...send a copy to his [her] section [clinic] chief. This complaint will also be included in the information we provide for the physicians' annual evaluations."

   b. [if other employee] "...send a copy to his/her supervisor for follow-up with him/her."

   c. [if system, such as cancer screening] "...send a copy to the director of that program for information."

2. "Is there anything else you would like done?"

III. Problem Solve

A. Review options

1. Wants to change primary care physician—transfer to Physician Selection

2. Wants a second opinion—transfer to the appropriate section/cluster for appointment scheduling

3. Refund of co-pay—follow guidelines developed by administration for doing this efficiently

4. Waive charges
   "I'll order your medical record, and then consult with members of the medical staff and administration. Based on their review, I'll find out if we can arrange the coverage exception [write-off] that you requested."

5. Wants outside bills paid—request copy of bills (itemized with procedure codes) and outside records. If bill is for more than $100, request patient/customer put complaint in writing.
   - "I'll order your medical record, and then consult with members of the medical staff and administration. Based on their review, I'll find out if we can arrange the coverage exception [write-off] that you requested."
   - "I'll also need a copy of the records of the care you received from the community physician [Elsewhere Memorial Hospital]. If you call that doctor and sign a release for those records, I'll start our review as soon as I receive those records."

6. Wants staff member fired
   "Personnel issues are the responsibility of the manager. We appreciate your comments and they will be included in our staff performance reviews. However, we cannot discuss disciplinary decisions because that is considered confidential employer/employee information."

7. Other; something unique to that person—review options with administrator or Patient Representative manager
   "I'd like to discuss this with members of our administration to determine the best way to handle this review."

B. Agree on next contact
   "I'm going to look into this for you and get back to you [time frame]—hopefully in 24 hours/up to 48 hours

IV. Respond/Refer

A. Contact patient/customer with information concerning customized resolution: e.g., change MD's, second opinion appointment, information re. care or need for follow-up

B. If complaint involved is "formal" quality-of-care review, send consumer written summary of findings

C. Contact physician/team to arrange for necessary care if

   1. Patient/customer needs assistance immediately (i.e., within 1–2 days)

   2. **and** patient/physician relationship is still reasonably intact

D. Contact clinic or section chief for assistance if

1. Patient/customer needs assistance immediately (i.e., within 1–2 days), **and** patient/physician relationship is significantly damaged

2. **or** If patient/customer is requesting referral to outside provider

3. **or** If care in question is confined to that one clinic or specialty

E. Coordinate review with appropriate medical director or chief of staff if

1. Review at previous two levels did not satisfy patient/customer

2. **or** Patient/customer is requesting retrospective review of care involving multiple facilities or specialties

3. **or** Patient/customer is requesting significant dollars

F. Notification of Risk Management

1. If there appears to be potential risk of exposure; e.g., loss of limb or permanent sensory deficit, delayed diagnosis with poor prognosis, patient is historically litigious or has conferred with an attorney

2. Transfer case to Risk Management if

a. Patient is requesting "pain and suffering" or "general compensation"

b. Failed sterilization

c. "Formal" quality-of-care review indicates care was appropriate and there are no nonclinical extenuating circumstances that can be appealed administratively

V. Follow-Up

A. For those complaints resolved by telephone, a follow-up letter should be sent that

1. Summarizes the patient/customer's request, the actions you took, and agreed-upon resolution

2. Apologizes for the patient/customer's feelings of dissatisfaction or inconvenience

3. Avoids using names of specific staff involved in the complaint if at all possible (you never know where these letters may go or who will see them)

4. Reports any system changes that have occurred as a result of this complaint

5. Offers to assist in the future if needed

B. Document complaint and distribute as appropriate

Appendix D

Service Recovery Protocols for Member Services Departments

Service Recovery, as described in Chapter 2, involves five basic steps. Below is a model for developing Service Recovery protocols. A centralized marketing/enrollment/member services-department, or a business office, receives calls from dissatisfied patient/customers. Staff in these areas will also need assistance in developing the appropriate Service Recovery responses. The following are some ideas for how these calls might be handled.

Model

I. Patient/Customer Contact
   A. Listen—focus on the patient/customer with attentive body language (if in person) and voice inflections (if over the telephone)
   B. Ask open-ended questions
   C. Empathize; validate the patient/customer's perspective
   D. Clarify the patient/customer's expectation for resolution

II. Acknowledge

    A. Apologize—without assigning blame or guilt

    B. Verify the facts

    C. Explain what you can do; provide general overview of the process you will follow to resolve the concern

    D. Agree on next contact
       "I'm going to look into this for you and get back to you [time frame]"—hopefully in 24 hours/up to 48 hours

III. Problem Solve

    A. Consult with others

       1. Exchange information

       2. Collect information for explaining resolution

       3. Identify options

       4. Together, ask what's the right thing to do; what can we do; what will we do

    B. Explore options

       1. Identify options

       2. Together, ask what's the right thing to do; what can we do; what will we do

    C. Update consumer if necessary

IV. Respond/Refer

    A. Contact patient/customer with customized resolution

    B. Transfer complaint, if appropriate, to another department/division/region etc.

       1. Contact the resource person and relay all the pertinent information and facts about the problem

       2. Negotiate with the resource person to assume responsibility for investigating, reviewing, and/or resolving the problem; determine who will notify the patient/customer with the final resolution

       3. Advise the patient/customer of the next step, including who the resource person is and how to reach him or her

       4. Document in writing the pertinent facts and the plan for resolution, and send a copy to the resource person

    C. Update patient/customer if necessary

V. Follow-Up

    A. Bring closure to complaint
       Summarize patient/customer's request, the actions you took, and agreed-upon resolution.

    B. Thank patient/customer

C. Share your organization's Service Recovery standards, if appropriate

    1. You strive to recognize the patient/customer as an individual

    2. You strive to provide the patient/customer with an easy, obvious process for sharing concerns

    3. You strive to provide the patient/customer with a key contact person

    4. You strive for a fair resolution

    5. You strive for a fast resolution

    6. You strive to provide consistent, clear, and accurate information

D. Written follow-up letter

    1. Summarize patient/customer's request, the actions you took, and agreed-upon resolution

    2. Apologize for the patient/customer's feelings of dissatisfaction or inconvenience

    3. Report any system changes that have occurred as a result of this complaint

    4. Offer to assist in the future if needed

E. Document complaint and distribute, if appropriate

Service Recovery Standards

85% of all complaints are resolved by the person who hears the complaint

85% of all complaints are resolved the same day

Complex complaints are resolved within two weeks

▼ Marketing Department/Business Office

Appointment Wait Time

I. Patient/Customer Contact

A. Listen—focus on the patient/customer with attentive body language (if in person) and voice inflections (if over the telephone)

B. Ask open-ended questions

    1. "Who have you talked to about this and when?"

    2. "What are your symptoms? Are these new or more severe since you were referred?"

    3. "Who is your primary care practice physician?"

    4. "What else has your physician recommended to treat this problem?"

    5. "What is your concern about waiting until _____?" (ask only if it's not clear why patient/customer can't wait—do not antagonize person further).

    6. "Is there anything else I need to be aware of?"

C. Empathize; validate the patient/customer's perspective

1. "I'm sure you must be . . ."

2. "I understand this is very frustrating for you."

3. "It sounds like you're . . ."

4. "I'm glad you let me/us know that . . ."

D. Clarify expectation for resolution

1. "When did you want to be seen?"

2. "When are you available—are there any times you cannot come for an appointment?"

3. "Would you be willing to go to another Plan facility in _____ or _____?"

II. Acknowledge

A. Apologize—without assigning blame or guilt

1. "I'm sorry this isn't convenient."

2. "I'm sorry this isn't what you were expecting."

B. Verify the facts
"Let me make sure I understand what you've told me . . ."

C. Explain what you can do; provide general overview of the process you will follow to resolve the concern

D. Agree on next contact
"I'm going to look into this for you and get back to you [time frame]—hopefully in 24 hours/up to 48 hours

III. Problem Solve

A. Consult with others

1. If primary care appointment access, call the primary care facility and discuss with the Patient Representative, and ask him or her to follow up with patient/customer

2. If specialty care and patient/customer accept referral urgency level:

   a. Call "head nurse" or nurse manager and request they follow up with patient/customer; or

   b. Call section chief or facility manager

3. If specialty care and patient/customer disagree with referral urgency level, call primary care facility and discuss with the Patient Representative, and ask him or her to follow up with patient/customer

B. Update patient/customer if necessary

IV. Respond/Refer

    A. Contact patient/customer with customized resolution

    B. Based on patient/customer's temperament, provide explanation of why the Plan schedules appointments the way it does

        1. Verify that appointment scheduling is driven by the triage process

        2. If waiting would adversely affect patient's condition, he or she would be seen earlier

    C. Transfer complaint, if appropriate, to another department/division/region etc.

        1. Contact the resource person and relay all the pertinent information and facts about the problem

        2. Negotiate with the resource person to assume responsibility for investigating, reviewing, and/or resolving the problem; determine who will notify the patient/customer with the final resolution

        3. Advise the patient/customer of the next step, including who the resource person is and how to reach him or her

        4. Document in writing the pertinent facts and the plan for resolution, and send a copy to the resource person

    D. Update patient/customer if necessary

V. Follow-Up

    A. Bring closure to complaint
       Summarize patient/customer's request, the actions you took, and agreed-upon resolution

    B. Thank patient/customer

    C. Share your organization's Service Recovery standards, if appropriate

        1. You strive to recognize the patient/customer as an individual

        2. You strive to provide the patient/customer with an easy, obvious process for sharing concerns

        3. You strive to provide the patient/customer with a key contact person

        4. You strive for a fair resolution

        5. You strive for a fast resolution

        6. You strive to provide consistent, clear, and accurate information

    D. Written follow-up letter

        1. Summarize patient/customer's request, the actions you took, and agreed-upon resolution

        2. Apologize for the patient/customer's feelings of dissatisfaction or inconvenience

3. Report any system changes that have occurred as a result of this complaint

4. Offer to assist in the future if needed

E. Document complaint and distribute, if appropriate

▼ Marketing Department/Business Office

Staff Attitude or Customer Service Orientation

I. Patient/Customer Contact

   A. Listen—focus on the patient/customer with attentive body language (if in person) and voice inflections (if over the telephone)

   B. Ask open-ended questions

     1. "Who said this to you? When?"

     2. "What specifically did he [she] say?"

     3. "Can you describe the situation in more detail for me?"

   C. Empathize; validate the patient/customer's perspective
"It sounds like that was a difficult [awkward/frustrating] situation for you."

II. Acknowledge

   A. Apologize—without assigning blame or guilt

     1. "I'm sorry you felt _____."

     2. "I'm sure it wasn't their intent to _____."

   B. Verify the facts

   C. Explain what you can do; provide general overview of the process you will follow to resolve the concern

     1. "I will be documenting your complaint and . . ."

       a. [If physician] ". . . sending a copy to his [her] section [clinic] chief."

       b. [If other employee] ". . . sending a copy to his [her] facility manager [supervisor] for follow-up with him [her]."

   D. Clarify expectation for resolution

     1. "Is there anything else you would like done?"

       a. Change primary care physician—transfer patient to clinic's Physician Selection

       b. Second opinion appointment—transfer to the appropriate section [cluster] for appointment scheduling

       c. Refund of co-pay—follow guidelines that office/department/division has developed for doing this efficiently

      d. Payment of outside bill—request consumer send a copy of bills (itemized with procedure codes) and outside records to you, and then forward to the appropriate administrative Patient Representative Department

  E. Agree on next contact

    1. "I'm going to look into this for you and get back to you [time frame]"—hopefully in 24 hours/up to 48 hours

    2. "I'm going to transfer you to Physician Selection [the _____ department/office] to change physicians [schedule an appointment]."

    3. "I will send you a medical records release form that you can sign and give to the community physician. His office will then send the records directly to me."

    4. "I will review this with the chief of staff/the clinic/the section, and get back to you [time frame]"—hopefully in 24 hours/up to 48 hours

III. Problem Solve

  A. Consult with others

    1. Exchange information

    2. Collect information for explaining resolution

    3. Identify options

    4. Together, ask what's the right thing to do; what can we do; what will we do

  B. Explore options

    1. Identify options

    2. Together, ask what's the right thing to do; what can we do; what will we do

  C. Update patient/customer if necessary

IV. Respond/Refer

  A. Contact patient/customer with customized resolution

  B. Educate staff—if patient was obnoxious, it is not okay for staff to retaliate; we have a responsibility to maintain professionalism

  C. Transfer complaint, if appropriate, to another department/division/region etc.

    1. Contact the resource person and relay all the pertinent information and facts about the problem

    2. Negotiate with the resource person to assume responsibility for investigating, reviewing, and/or resolving the problem; determine who will notify the patient/customer with the final resolution

    3. Advise the patient/customer of the next step, including who the resource person is and how to reach him or her

    4. Document in writing the pertinent facts and the plan for resolution, and send a copy to the resource person

D. Update patient/customer, if necessary

V. Follow-Up

A. Bring closure to complaint
Summarize patient/customer's request, the actions you took, and agreed-upon resolution

B. Thank patient/customer

C. Written follow-up letter

1. Summarize patient/customer's request, the actions you took, and agreed-upon resolution

2. Apologize for the patient/customer's feelings of dissatisfaction or inconvenience

3. Report any system changes that have occurred as a result of this complaint

4. Offer to assist in the future if needed

D. Document complaint and distribute, as appropriate

▼ Marketing Department/Business Office
Disputed Billing

I. Patient/Customer Contact

A. Listen—focus on the patient/customer with attentive body language (if in person) and voice inflections (if over the telephone)

B. Empathize; validate the patient/customer's perspective
"I can understand your frustration."

C. Ask open-ended questions

1. "When did you receive the service? Where?"

2. "Did you talk to anyone about the possibility that the service would not be covered? Who?"

3. "Why do you think the bill is in error?"

4. "What information have your received about your benefits?"

5. "May I have your middle initial and the spelling of your last name . . . what is your patient number?"

II. Acknowledge

A. Apologize—without assigning blame or guilt

1. "I'm sorry this bill is so upsetting to you."

2. "I'm sorry you thought this was a covered service."

B. Verify the facts

"Let me see if I understand what happened . . ."

C. Explain what you can do; provide general overview of the process you will follow to resolve the concern

" I'd be happy to help you with this. Let me check into this and get back to you with the information I learn."

D. Agree on next contact

"I'm going to look into this for you and get back to you [time frame]"—hopefully in 24 hours/up to 48 hours

III. Problem Solve

A. Consult with others—Medical Accounts Receivable

1. Exchange information—received bill because

a. Coverage not effective on date of service

b. Medical condition was determined to be a noncovered service

c. Service was cosmetic

2. Collect information for explaining resolution

3. Identify options

4. Together, ask what's the right thing to do; what can we do; what will we do

B. Explore and identify options

1. If charges are appropriate, can payment arrangements be made?

2. If payment creates a financial hardship, is patient/customer eligible for social assistance fund?

C. Update patient/customer if necessary

IV. Respond/Refer

A. Contact patient/customer with customized resolution

1. "I learned that you received a bill for those services because _____. The information that these services aren't covered is in the Certificate of Coverage mailed to you on _____. Would you like me to send you another copy?"

2. "You received a bill because those services were for [condition], which was identified as a noncovered condition. If you disagree with that determination, you can appeal it."

3. "When I was researching your concern, I found that you are not covered by this Plan. I suggest you contact your personnel department to look into it for you."

B. Transfer complaint, if appropriate, to another department/division/region etc.

1. Contact the resource person, and relay all the pertinent information and facts about the problem

2. Negotiate with the resource person to assume responsibility for investigating, reviewing, and/or resolving the problem; determine who will notify the patient/customer with the final resolution

3. Advise the patient/customer of the next step, including who the resource person is and how to reach him or her

4. Document in writing the pertinent facts and the plan for resolution, and send a copy to the resource person

C. Update patient/customer if necessary

V. Follow-Up

A. Bring closure to complaint
Summarize patient/customer's request, the actions you took, and agreed-upon resolution

B. Thank patient/customer

1. "Thank you for calling us, and I'm sorry this was confusing to sort out. I appreciate your patience while we researched your coverage status."

2. "Thank you for calling us, and I'm sorry we weren't able to help you."

C. Share your organization's Service Recovery standards, if appropriate

1. You strive to recognize the patient/customer as an individual

2. You strive to provide the patient/customer with an easy, obvious process for sharing concerns

3. You strive to provide the patient/customer with a key contact person

4. You strive for a fair resolution

5. You strive for a fast resolution

6. You strive to provide consistent, clear, and accurate information

D. Written follow-up letter

1. Summarize patient/customer's request, the actions you took, and agreed-upon resolution

2. Apologize for the patient/customer's feelings of dissatisfaction or inconvenience

3. Report any system changes that have occurred as a result of this complaint

4. Offer to assist in the future if needed

E. Document complaint and distribute, if appropriate

▼ Marketing Department/Business Office
Co-Payments

I. Patient/Customer Contact

    A. Listen—focus on the patient/customer with attentive body language (if in person) and voice inflections (if over the telephone)

    B. Ask open-ended questions—be careful not to offend caller
"Can you tell me a little more about your concern?"

    C. Empathize; validate the patient/customer's perspective
"I understand your concern. Healthcare costs are rising above the rate of inflation."

    D. Clarify expectation for resolution

        1. Is patient/customer "venting" without expectation that anything can be done about it?

        2. Does patient/customer need financial assistance with premiums?

II. Acknowledge

    A. Apologize—without assigning blame or guilt
"I am sorry this is creating a hardship for you."

    B. Verify the facts
"Because of the increase are you unable to get your medication [**or** see your physician]?"

    C. Explain what you can do; provide general overview of the process you will follow to resolve the concern

        1. "I am documenting your concern and forwarding this information to the [name] department. Your comments and those of other consumers will be shared with the Plan administrators."

        2. "I am documenting your concern and will share it with the people who negotiate the contract with your employer. Please understand, however, that all the plans have these co-pays now."

        3. Explain what the Plan is doing to keep costs down

III. Problem Solve

    A. Explore options
"You may be eligible for other programs that could help you with the extra costs."

    B. Update patient/customer if necessary

IV. Respond/Refer

    A. Transfer complaint, if appropriate, to Member Services Department for further action or assistance

1. Contact the resource person, and relay all the pertinent information and facts about the problem

2. Negotiate with the resource person to assume responsibility for investigating, reviewing, and/or resolving the problem; determine who will notify the patient/customer with the final resolution

3. Advise the patient/customer of the next step, including who the resource person is and how to reach him or her

4. Document in writing the pertinent facts and the plan for resolution, and send a copy to the resource person

B. Update patient/customer if necessary

V. Follow-Up

A. Bring closure to complaint
Summarize patient/customer's request, the actions you took, and agreed-upon resolution

B. Thank patient/customer

C. Share your organization's Service Recovery standards, if appropriate

1. You strive to recognize the patient/customer as an individual

2. You strive to provide the patient/customer with an easy, obvious process for sharing concerns

3. You strive to provide the patient/customer with a key contact person

4. You strive for a fair resolution

5. You strive for a fast resolution

6. You strive to provide consistent, clear, and accurate information

D. Written follow-up letter

1. Summarize patient/customer's request, the actions you took, and agreed-upon resolution

2. Apologize for the patient/customer's feelings of dissatisfaction or inconvenience

3. Report any system changes that have occurred as a result of this complaint

4. Offer to assist in the future if needed

E. Document complaint and distribute, if appropriate

▼ Marketing Department/Business Office

Incorrect Personal Data in System

I. Patient/Customer Contact

A. Listen—focus on the patient/customer with attentive body language (if in person) and voice inflections (if over the telephone)

B. Empathize; validate the patient/customer's perspective
"I can understand your frustration."

C. Ask open-ended questions

1. "May I have your Plan patient number [**or** first name, middle initial, and the spelling of your last name, and the month and year of your birth]?"

2. "Which information is incorrect?"

II. Acknowledge

A. Apologize—without assigning blame or guilt

1. "I'm sorry your first contact with us was so disappointing [upsetting etc.]."

2. "I'm sorry you've had difficulty."

B. Verify the facts
"Let me see if I understand what happened . . ."

C. Explain what you can do; provide general overview of the process you will follow to resolve the concern

1. "I'd be happy to help you with this. I will contact Membership Services this morning [afternoon] to make these changes. If there is a problem, I will have them call you directly."

2. "You should receive a corrected ID card in the next ten days."

D. Agree on next contact
"If the people in Member Services have any questions, they will call you directly. If you don't receive your new card by [date], please call me. My name is _____ , I work in the [name] Department, and my phone number is ____–_____."

III. Problem Solve

A. Consult with others—Member Services Department
1. Verify correct information
2. Request that it be corrected

B. Update patient/customer if necessary

IV. Respond/Refer

A. Contact patient/customer with customized resolution
"When I was researching your concern, I found that your enrollment card said _____. I suggest you contact your personnel department to put through a correction."

B. Transfer complaint, if appropriate, to another department/division/region etc.

1. Contact the resource person, and relay all the pertinent information and facts about the problem

2. Negotiate with the resource person to assume responsibility for investigating, reviewing, and/or resolving the problem; determine who will notify the patient/customer with the final resolution

3. Advise the patient/customer of the next step, including who the resource person is and how to reach him or her

4. Document in writing the pertinent facts and the plan for resolution, and send a copy to the resource person

C. Update patient/customer if necessary

V. Follow-Up

A. Bring closure to complaint
Summarize patient/customer's request, the actions you took, and agreed-upon resolution

B. Thank patient/customer
"Thank you for calling us, and I'm sorry this was confusing to sort out. I appreciate your patience while we researched this."

C. Share your organization's Service Recovery standards, if appropriate

1. You strive to recognize the patient/customer as an individual

2. You strive to provide the patient/customer with an easy, obvious process for sharing concerns

3. You strive to provide the patient/customer with a key contact person

4. You strive for a fair resolution

5. You strive for a fast resolution

6. You strive to provide consistent, clear, and accurate information

D. Written follow-up letter

1. Summarize patient/customer's request, the actions you took, and agreed-upon resolution

2. Apologize for the patient/customer's feelings of dissatisfaction or inconvenience

3. Report any system changes that have occurred as a result of this complaint

4. Offer to assist in the future if needed

E. Document complaint and distribute, if appropriate

▼ Marketing Department/Business Office

Insurance Enrollment Card Request

I. Patient/Customer Contact

A. Listen—focus on the patient/customer with attentive body language (if in person) and voice inflections (if over the telephone)

B. Empathize; validate the patient/customer's perspective

    1. "I can understand your frustration at not receiving your card."

    2. "I can understand how frustrating it would be to lose your wallet."

  C. Ask open-ended questions

    1. "May I have your first name, middle initial, and the spelling of your last name, and your month and year of birth?"

    2. "Do you know what your Plan patient number is?"

II. Acknowledge

  A. Apologize—without assigning blame or guilt

    1. "I'm sorry your first contact with us was so disappointing/upsetting/etc."

    2. "I'm sorry you've had difficulty."

  B. Verify the facts

    "Let me see if I understand what happened . . ."

  C. Explain what you can do; provide general overview of the process you will follow to resolve the concern

    1. "I'd be happy to help you with this. Let me check to see if we received an enrollment card from your employer. I'll verify your coverage and call you with your consumer number. We can then help you get scheduled for an appointment, even though you don't have your ID card(s) yet."

    2. "I'd be happy to help you with this. I'll put in a request for a new card this morning [afternoon], and you should receive it in the next ten days."

  D. Agree on next contact

    1. "If you don't receive the card(s) by date, please call me back. My name is _____, I work in the (name) Department, and my telephone number here is ____–_____."

    2. "If we don't have an enrollment card on file, I will call you back. You will then need to contact your personnel [benefits] office to complete one."

III. Problem Solve

  A. Consult with others—Member Services Courtesy Line

    1. Exchange information—may not have ID number/card because:

      a. Not eligible due to

        • Employer's probationary period

        • Have other carrier coverage through employer

        • Coverage not effective yet

      b. Eligible but enrollment form not yet received

    2. Collect information for explaining resolution

B. Explore options

  1. Identify options

    a. If patient/customer needs care *now,* agree to see patient although coverage not yet effective, with understanding that he will be billed for the services

    b. Assist with seeking care in the community if it is determined person is not eligible, and will not be eligible for Plan coverage in the near future

C. Update patient/customer if necessary

IV. Respond/Refer

  A. Contact patient/customer with customized resolution

    1. "Your patient number is _____, and I can transfer you to your medical center's physician selection person to choose a physician and to schedule an appointment; or, I can give you the number for you to call at your convenience."

    2. "You will be receiving your ID card within ____ days. If you do not receive it, please call me back. My name is _____, and my number is ____–_____."

    3. "When I was researching your concern, I found that you are not covered by the Plan at this time. I suggest you contact your personnel department to look into it for you."

    4. "Because you need medical care and will not have coverage through this Plan, my suggestion is that you contact the community Physician Referral service. They have information about community physicians, such as if they are Board certified, and if they accept your insurance."

  B. Transfer complaint, if appropriate, to another department/division/region etc.

    1. Contact the resource person, and relay all the pertinent information and facts about the problem

    2. Negotiate with the resource person to assume responsibility for investigating, reviewing, and/or resolving the problem; determine who will notify the patient/customer with the final resolution

    3. Advise the patient/customer of the next step, including who the resource person is and how to reach him or her

    4. Document in writing the pertinent facts and the plan for resolution, and send a copy to the resource person

  C. Update consumer if necessary

V. Follow-Up

  A. Bring closure to complaint
Summarize patient/customer's request, the actions you took, and agreed-upon resolution

B. Thank consumer

1. "Thank you for calling us, and I'm sorry this was confusing to sort out. I appreciate your patience while we researched your coverage status."

2. "Thank you for calling us, and I'm sorry we weren't able to see you. I hope that if you have the opportunity to choose our Plan in the future, you will consider joining us."

C. Share your organization's Service Recovery standards, if appropriate

1. You strive to recognize the patient/customer as an individual

2. You strive to provide the patient/customer with an easy, obvious process for sharing concerns

3. You strive to provide the patient/customer with a key contact person

4. You strive for a fair resolution

5. You strive for a fast resolution

6. You strive to provide consistent, clear, and accurate information

D. Written follow-up letter

1. Summarize patient/customer's request, the actions you took, and agreed-upon resolution

2. Apologize for the patient/customer's feelings of dissatisfaction or inconvenience

3. Report any system changes that have occurred as a result of this complaint

4. Offer to assist in the future if needed

E. Document complaint and distribute, if appropriate

▼ Member Services/Marketing Department/Business Office

Lack of Complete Information about Coverage

I. Patient/Customer Contact

A. Listen—focus on the patient/customer with attentive body language (if in person) and voice inflections (if over the telephone)

B. Empathize; validate the patient/customer's perspective
"I can understand your frustration."

C. Ask open-ended questions

1. "Who did you talk to about this?"

2. "What information did they give you?"

3. "Have you received the care [service] yet?"

4. "May I have your patient number [**or** first name, middle initial, and the spelling of your last name, and your month and year of birth]?"

II. Acknowledge

    A. Apologize—without assigning blame or guilt

        1. "I'm sorry you feel you were not given accurate [complete] information."

        2. "I'm sorry you've had difficulty."

    B. Verify the facts
       "Let me see if I understand what happened . . ."

    C. Explain what you can do; provide general overview of the process you will follow to resolve the concern

        1. "I'd be happy to help you with this. I can send you some additional information about your benefits [how to receive services]. Where shall I send this material?"

        2. "Perhaps it would be helpful to talk to someone who works in the clinic about how to receive care. When would be a good time for them to call you?"

    D. Agree on next contact

        1. "I'm going to send this information to you in tomorrow morning's mail."

        2. "I'm going to contact the Patient Representative at the _____ clinic and ask her [him] to call you. I can let her [him] know some of the problems you've had already. Or I can give you the number and you can call when it's a good time for you. Which would you prefer?"

III. Problem Solve

    A. Consult with others

        1. If the patient/customer obtained noncovered services based on the misinformation [lack of complete information], contact the Regional [Division] Patient Representative staff to determine who should follow up with the patient/customer

        2. If the patient/customer has not yet received noncovered services, verify [clarify] the coverage of the service, and report the misinformation [lack of complete information] to the appropriate department or facility manager

    B. Update patient/customer if necessary

IV. Respond/Refer

    A. Contact patient/customer with customized resolution

        1. "I was able to confirm that _____ is not a covered service under your plan. I also contacted _____ at _____, and they will be following up with you. They may ask you to put your complaint in writing so they can review your request for an administrative decision to cover the bill. Their phone number is _____–_____."

    2. "I was able to confirm that _____ is not a covered service under your plan. Have you talked to your physician about other treatments that might be helpful for you?"

  B. Transfer complaint, if appropriate, to another department/division/region etc.

    1. Contact the resource person and relay all the pertinent information and facts about the problem

    2. Negotiate with the resource person to assume responsibility for investigating, reviewing, and/or resolving the problem, including who will notify the patient/customer with the final resolution

    3. Advise the patient/customer of the next step, including who the resource person is and how to reach him or her

    4. Document in writing the pertinent facts and the plan for resolution, and send a copy to the resource person

  C. Update patient/customer if necessary

V. Follow-Up

  A. Bring closure to complaint
    Summarize patient/customer's request, the actions you took, and agreed-upon resolution

  B. Thank patient/customer

    1. "Thank you for calling us, and I'm sorry this was confusing to sort out. I appreciate your patience while we researched your coverage questions."

    2. "Thank you for calling us, and I'm sorry we weren't able to help you with this question."

  C. Share your organization's Service Recovery standards, if appropriate

    1. You strive to recognize the patient/customer as an individual

    2. You strive to provide the patient/customer with an easy, obvious process for sharing concerns

    3. You strive to provide the patient/customer with a key contact person

    4. You strive for a fair resolution

    5. You strive for a fast resolution

    6. You strive to provide consistent, clear, and accurate information

  D. Written follow-up letter

    1. Summarize patient/customer's request, the actions you took, and agreed-upon resolution

    2. Apologize for the patient/customer's feelings of dissatisfaction or inconvenience

    3. Report any system changes that have occurred as a result of this complaint

4. Offer to assist in the future if needed

E. Document complaint and distribute, if appropriate

▼ Marketing Department/Business Office

Enrollment Status Dispute

I. Patient/Customer Contact

   A. Listen—focus on the patient/customer with attentive body language (if in person) and voice inflections (if over the telephone)

   B. Empathize; validate the patient/customer's perspective
"I can understand your frustration."

   C. Ask open-ended questions

      1. "Where were you denied services?"

      2. "Who is your employer?"

      3. "Do you know when your coverage began?"

      4. "Did you fill out an enrollment card [form]?"

      5. "May I have your middle initial and the spelling of your last name?"

II. Acknowledge

   A. Apologize—without assigning blame or guilt

      1. "I'm sorry your first contact with us was so disappointing [upsetting, etc.]."

      2. "I'm sorry you've had difficulty."

   B. Verify the facts
"Let me see if I understand what happened . . ."

   C. Explain what you can do; provide general overview of the process you will follow to resolve the concern
"I'd be happy to help you with this. Let me check to see if we received an enrollment card from your employer. I'll verify your coverage and call you with your patient number. We can then help you get scheduled for an appointment even though you don't have your ID card(s) yet."

   D. Agree on next contact

      1. "I'm going to look into this for you and get back to you [time frame]"—hopefully in 24 hours/up to 48 hours

      2. "If we don't have an enrollment card on file, you will need to contact your personnel [benefits] office to complete one."

III. Problem Solve

    A. Consult with others—Member Services Department

        1. Exchange information—may not have ID number [card] because

            a. Not eligible due to

- Employer's probationary period
- Other carrier coverage through employer
- Coverage not effective yet

            b. Eligible but enrollment form not yet received

        2. Collect information for explaining resolution

        3. Identify options

        4. Together, ask what's the right thing to do; what can we do; what will we do

    B. Explore options

        1. Identify options

            a. If patient/customer needs care *now*, agree to see patient although coverage not yet effective, with understanding that we will bill for the services

            b. Assist with seeking care in the community

        2. Together, ask what's the right thing to do; what can we do; what will we do

    C. Update patient/customer if necessary

IV. Respond/Refer

    A. Contact patient/customer with customized resolution

        1. "Your patient number is _____, and I can transfer you to your medical center's physician selection person to choose a physician and to schedule an appointment; or I can give you the number for you to call at your convenience."

        2. "You will be receiving your ID card within ____ days. If you do not receive it, please call me back. My name is _____, and my number is ____–_____."

        3. "When I was researching your concern, I found that you are not covered by this Plan at this time. I suggest you contact your personnel [benefits] department to look into it for you."

        4. "Because you need medical care, my suggestion is that you contact the community Physician Referral service. They have information about community physicians, such as if they are Board certified, and if they accept your insurance."

B. Transfer complaint, if appropriate, to another department/division/region etc.

1. Contact the resource person, and relay all the pertinent information and facts about the problem

2. Negotiate with the resource person to assume responsibility for investigating, reviewing, and/or resolving the problem; determine who will notify the patient/customer with the final resolution

3. Advise the patient/customer of the next step, including who the resource person is and how to reach him or her

4. Document in writing the pertinent facts and the plan for resolution, and send a copy to the resource person

C. Update patient/consumer if necessary

V. Follow-Up

A. Bring closure to complaint
   Summarize patient/customer's request, the actions you took, and agreed-upon resolution

B. Thank patient/customer

1. "Thank you for calling us, and I'm sorry this was confusing to sort out. I appreciate your patience while we researched your coverage status."

2. "Thank you for calling us, and I'm sorry we weren't able to see you. I hope that if you have the opportunity to choose our Plan in the future, you will consider joining us."

C. Share your organization's Service Recovery standards, if appropriate

1. You strive to recognize the patient/customer as an individual

2. You strive to provide the patient/customer with an easy, obvious process for sharing concerns

3. You strive to provide the patient/customer with a key contact person

4. You strive for a fair resolution

5. You strive for a fast resolution

6. You strive to provide consistent, clear, and accurate information

D. Written follow-up letter

1. Summarize patient/customer's request, the actions you took, and agreed-upon resolution

2. Apologize for the patient/customer's feelings of dissatisfaction or inconvenience

3. Report any system changes that have occurred as a result of this complaint

4. Offer to assist in the future if needed

E. Document complaint and distribute, if appropriate

▼ Marketing Department/Business Office
Referral Process—Internal/External

I. Patient/Customer Contact

    A. Listen—focus on the patient/customer with attentive body language (if in person) and voice inflections (if over the telephone)

    B. Empathize; validate the patient/customer's perspective
"I can understand your frustration."

    C. Ask open-ended questions

        1. "Which physician wrote the referral? When?"

        2. "Who were you being referred to [specialty]? For what condition?"

II. Acknowledge

    A. Apologize—without assigning blame or guilt

        1. "I'm sorry this has been so frustrating for you."

        2. "I'm sorry you've had difficulty arranging an appointment."

    B. Verify the facts
"Let me see if I understand what happened . . ."

    C. Explain what you can do; provide general overview of the process you will follow to resolve the concern
"I'd be happy to help you with this. Let me check into this, and either I or someone from your medical center will contact you."

    D. Agree on next contact
"I'm going to look into this for you and get back to you [time frame]"—hopefully in 24 hours/up to 48 hours

III. Problem Solve

    A. Consult with others—contact referring physician's nurse and share problem with her [him]
Exchange information—confirm information given you by the patient

    B. Explore and identify options

        1. Rewrite referral

        2. Contact specialty services manager for assistance in scheduling

        3. Contact referral services department to facilitate external referral

    C. Update patient/customer if necessary

IV. Respond/Refer

    A. Contact patient/customer with customized resolution
"I discussed your situation with _____, Dr. _____'s nurse. She will

have Dr. _____ write another referral, and will work with the specialty [referral services] manager to get that taken care of for you."

B. Transfer complaint, if appropriate, to another department/division/region etc.

   1. Contact the resource person, and relay all the pertinent information and facts about the problem

   2. Negotiate with the resource person to assume responsibility for investigating, reviewing, and/or resolving the problem; determine who will notify the patient/customer with the final resolution

   3. Advise the patient/customer of the next step, including who the resource person is and how to reach him or her

   4. Document in writing the pertinent facts and the plan for resolution, and send a copy to the resource person

C. Update patient/customer if necessary

V. Follow-Up

   A. Bring closure to complaint
      Summarize patient/customer's request, the actions you took, and agreed-upon resolution

   B. Thank patient/customer

      1. "Thank you for calling us, and I'm sorry you had trouble scheduling this appointment."

      2. "Thank you for calling me, and letting me help you with this matter."

   C. Share your organization's Service Recovery standards, if appropriate

      1. You strive to recognize the patient/customer as an individual

      2. You strive to provide the patient/customer with an easy, obvious process for sharing concerns

      3. You strive to provide the patient/customer with a key contact person

      4. You strive for a fair resolution

      5. You strive for a fast resolution

      6. You strive to provide consistent, clear, and accurate information

   D. Written follow-up letter

      1. Summarize patient/customer's request, the actions you took, and agreed-upon resolution

      2. Apologize for the patient/customer's feelings of dissatisfaction or inconvenience

      3. Report any system changes that have occurred as a result of this complaint

      4. Offer to assist in the future if needed

   E. Document complaint and distribute, if appropriate

▼ Marketing Department/Business Office
Termination of Coverage

I. Patient/Customer Contact

    A. Listen—focus on the patient/customer with attentive body language (if in person) and voice inflections (if over the telephone)

    B. Empathize; validate the patient/customer's perspective
"I can understand your frustration."

    C. Ask open-ended questions

        1. "Where were you denied services?"

        2. "Who is your employer?"

        3. "Do you know when your coverage is supposed to end?"

        4. "May I have your middle initial and the spelling of your last name, and your Plan patient number?"

II. Acknowledge

    A. Apologize—without assigning blame or guilt

        1. "I'm sorry this was so upsetting [embarrassing, etc.]."

        2. "I'm sorry you've had difficulty."

    B. Verify the facts
"Let me see if I understand what happened . . ."

    C. Explain what you can do; provide general overview of the process you will follow to resolve the concern
"I'd be happy to help you with this. Let me check to see what we received from your employer. I'll verify the effective dates of your coverage and call you back with that information."

    D. Agree on next contact

        1. "I'm going to look into this for you and get back to you [time frame]"—hopefully in 24 hours/up to 48 hours

        2. "In the meantime, I can call the pharmacy [clinic, etc.] and ask them to give you the prescription [see you, etc.] with the understanding that if your coverage has in fact ended, you will be billed for the service."

III. Problem Solve

    A. Consult with others—Member Services Information Line

        1. Exchange information

            a. Delinquency by consumer

            b. Delinquency by employer

            c. Terminated by employer

2. Collect information for explaining resolution

3. Identify options

    a. COBRA? Individual and Family plan?

    b. Pay retroactive premium

    c. Has the enrollee/dependent received services since effective date of termination for which they should expect a billing?

4. Together, ask what's the right thing to do; what can we do; what will we do

B. Explore options

1. Identify options

    a. If patient/customer needs care *now*, agree to see patient although coverage may be terminated, with understanding that we will bill for the services

    b. Assist with seeking care in the community

2. Together, ask what's the right thing to do; what can we do; what will we do

C. Update patient/customer if necessary

IV. Respond/Refer

A. Contact patient/customer with customized resolution

1. "It appears we did not receive premiums for the months of _____, _____, and _____. If you can send us a payment for $_____ by [date], we can reinstate your coverage."

2. "It appears your employer has not paid the premiums for your group since _____. Did you or your family receive any services during this time? We can set you up on an individual plan for $_____, which will give you continuous coverage."

3. "When I was researching your concern, I found that your employer terminated your coverage, effective [date]. I suggest you contact your personnel [benefits] department to look into it for you."

4. "Because you need medical care, my suggestion is that you contact the community physician referral service. They have information about community physicians, such as if they are Board certified, and if they accept your insurance."

B. Transfer complaint, if appropriate, to another department/division/region etc.

1. Contact the resource person and relay all the pertinent information and facts about the problem

2. Negotiate with the resource person to assume responsibility for investigating, reviewing, and/or resolving the problem; determine who will notify the patient/customer with the final resolution

3. Advise the patient/customer of the next step, including who the resource person is and how to reach him or her

4. Document in writing the pertinent facts and the plan for resolution, and send a copy to the resource person

C. Update patient/customer if necessary

V. Follow-Up

A. Bring closure to complaint
Summarize patient/customer's request, the actions you took, and agreed-upon resolution

B. Thank patient/customer

1. "Thank you for calling us, and I'm sorry this was confusing to sort out. I appreciate your patience while we researched your coverage status."

2. "Thank you for calling us, and I'm sorry we weren't able to help you. I hope that if you have the opportunity to choose our Plan in the future, you will consider joining us."

C. Share your organization's Service Recovery standards, if appropriate

1. You strive to recognize the patient/customer as an individual

2. You strive to provide the patient/customer with an easy, obvious process for sharing concerns

3. You strive to provide the patient/customer with a key contact person

4. You strive for a fair resolution

5. You strive for a fast resolution

6. You strive to provide consistent, clear, and accurate information

D. Written follow-up letter

1. Summarize patient/customer's request, the actions you took, and agreed-upon resolution

2. Apologize for the patient/customer's feelings of dissatisfaction or inconvenience

3. Report any system changes that have occurred as a result of this complaint

4. Offer to assist in the future if needed

E. Document complaint and distribute, if appropriate

Service Recovery Protocols for Home Health Agencies

Service Recovery, as described in Chapter 2, involves five basic steps. The following is a model for developing service recovery protocols for home health agencies, as well as examples of scripting for problems received by agency staff.

Model

I. Patient/Customer Contact

    A. Listen—focus on the patient/customer with attentive body language (if in person) and voice inflections (if over the telephone)

    B. Ask open-ended questions

    C. Empathize; validate the patient/customer's perspective

    D. Clarify the patient/customer's expectation for resolution

II. Acknowledge

    A. Apologize—without assigning blame or guilt

    B. Verify the facts

    C. Explain what you can do; provide general overview of the process you will follow to resolve the concern

D. Agree on next contact
"I'm going to look into this for you and get back to you [time frame]"—hopefully in 24 hours/up to 48 hours

III. Problem Solve

A. Consult with others

1. Exchange information

2. Collect information for explaining resolution

3. Identify options

4. Together, ask what's the right thing to do; what can we do; what will we do

B. Explore options

1. Identify options

2. Together, ask what's the right thing to do; what can we do; what will we do

C. Update consumer if necessary

IV. Respond/Refer

A. Contact patient/customer with customized resolution

B. Transfer complaint, if appropriate, to another department/division/region etc.

1. Contact the resource person, and relay all the pertinent information and facts about the problem

2. Negotiate with the resource person to assume responsibility for investigating, reviewing, and/or resolving the problem; determine who will notify the patient/customer with the final resolution

3. Advise the patient/customer of the next step, including who the resource person is and how to reach him or her

4. Document in writing the pertinent facts and the plan for resolution, and send a copy to the resource person

C. Update patient/customer if necessary

V. Follow-Up

A. Bring closure to complaint
Summarize patient/customer's request, the actions you took, and agreed-upon resolution

B. Thank patient/customer

C. Share your organization's Service Recovery standards, if appropriate

1. You strive to recognize the patient/customer as an individual

2. You strive to provide the patient/customer with an easy, obvious process for sharing concerns

3. You strive to provide the patient/customer with a key contact person

4. You strive for a fair resolution

5. You strive for a fast resolution

6. You strive to provide consistent, clear, and accurate information

D. Written follow-up letter

1. Summarize patient/customer's request, the actions you took, and agreed-upon resolution

2. Apologize for the patient/customer's feelings of dissatisfaction or inconvenience

3. Report any system changes that have occurred as a result of this complaint

4. Offer to assist in the future if needed

E. Document complaint and distribute, if appropriate

Service Recovery Standards

85% of all complaints are resolved by the person who hears the complaint

85% of all complaints are resolved the same day

Complex complaints are resolved within two weeks

▼ Home Health Agency Staff: Receptionist

Clinician Late for Appointment

Note: The best way to avoid this complaint is to anticipate the problem and give patient/customers the option of waiting or rescheduling before they begin to complain. This requires frequent communication from providers in the field and the office.

I. Patient/Customer Contact

A. Listen—focus on the patient/customer with appropriate voice inflections

B. Empathize; validate the patient/customer's perspective
"I see your appointment was supposed to be at 3:15. It can be frustrating to wait for someone to arrive."

II. Acknowledge

A. Apologize—without assigning blame or guilt
"I'm sorry we've delayed you."

B. Explain what you can do; provide general overview of the process you will follow to resolve the concern

1. "Andrea spent longer than expected with another patient this afternoon."

2. "It will probably be at least another half hour before she arrives. Will that work for you, or would you prefer to reschedule for another day?"

III. Follow-Up

    A. Bring closure to complaint

        1. Summarize patient/customer's request, the actions you took, and agreed-upon resolution

        Note: Make every effort to reschedule the patient for the earliest date possible—do not add insult to injury

    B. Thank patient/customer
    "I appreciate your telling me about this. I know it's frustrating to have to wait. We try to stay on schedule, but sometimes the RN [PT, aides, etc.] are delayed."

    C. Share your organization's Service Recovery standards, if appropriate

        1. You strive to recognize the patient/customer as an individual

        2. You strive to provide the patient/customer with an easy, obvious process for sharing concerns

        3. You strive to provide the patient/customer with a key contact person

        4. You strive for a fair resolution

        5. You strive for a fast resolution

        6. You strive to provide consistent, clear, and accurate information

    D. Offer to assist in the future if needed
    "In case you have any questions later, here's my name and the office phone number."

    E. Document complaint and distribute, if appropriate

▼ Home Health Agency Staff: Clinician

Late for Appointment

Note: A clinician can fall behind schedule for a variety of reasons, such as patients with unexpected treatment needs or heavy traffic. If the clinician falls more than fifteen minutes behind schedule, good customer service requires she contact the office so her other patients can be notified and given the option of waiting for her or rescheduling. If, however, clinicians always run late because the scheduling is too tight, then a team should be assigned to study the problem.

    I. Patient/Customer Contact

        A. Listen—focus on the patient/customer with attentive body language (if in person). If this is the first visit, come into the house, shake the patient's hand [and others who are present] and introduce yourself.

II. Acknowledge

    A. Apologize—without assigning blame or guilt

        1. "I'm sorry you had to wait."

        2. "I'm sorry I was delayed. I hope this hasn't upset your schedule for today."

    B. Verify the facts

        1. "The patient scheduled just before you turned out to have more serious problems than we expected, and I had to spend more time with her." (*Note:* The patient will usually interpret this to mean that you will spend the time necessary to assure she receives good care.)

        2. "I was caught in the construction on Highway 99, and even the back roads had heavy traffic."

    C. Explain what you can do; provide general overview of the process you will follow to resolve the concern
"I know my office called to let you know I was going to be late. Do you still have time to see me today, or do you need to reschedule?"

III. Follow-Up
Thank patient/customer

        1. "I appreciate your understanding and patience today."

        2. "Thank you for being so understanding."

▼ Home Health Agency Staff

Quality of Care

I. Patient/Customer Contact

    A. Listen—focus on the patient/customer with attentive body language (if in person) and voice inflections (if over the telephone)

    B. Empathize; validate the patient/customer's perspective

        1. "It must be frustrating to feel that you're not getting better."

        2. "It sounds like this has been a difficult time for you."

II. Acknowledge

    A. Apologize—without assigning blame or guilt

        1. "I'm sorry you're unhappy with your care."

        2. "I'm sorry you're still having health problems."

    B. Explain what you can do; provide general overview of the process you will follow to resolve the concern

       "I will document your concern and share it with Ms. Smith, our clinical care supervisor. I can also arrange for a different RN [PT, aide, etc.] to see you."

    C. Agree on next contact

       "Ms. Smith is the best person to follow up with you on this. Would you like her to call you back?"

III. Problem Solve

    A. Consult with others: exchange information

    B. Update consumer if necessary

IV. Follow-Up

    A. Bring closure to complaint

       Summarize patient/customer's request, the actions you took, and agreed-upon resolution

    B. Thank patient/customer

       "Thank you for sharing your concerns with me. We want you to have confidence in the care you receive from us."

▼ Home Health Agency Staff

Disputed Billing

I. Patient/Customer Contact

    A. Listen—focus on the patient/customer with attentive body language (if in person) and voice inflections (if over the telephone)

    B. Empathize; validate the patient/customer's perspective

       "I can understand your frustration."

    C. Ask open-ended questions

       1. "When does the bill say you received the service?"

       2. "Did you talk to anyone about the possibility that the service would not be covered? Who?"

       3. "Why do you think the bill is in error?"

       4. "What information have you received about your benefits?"

       5. "Did your copy of Dr. Jones' referral specify how many visits you were supposed to have?"

       6. "Did your copy of Dr. Jones' referral say anything about treatment for this condition?"

       7. "May I have your middle initial and the spelling of your last name? What is your patient number?"

II. Acknowledge

    A. Apologize—without assigning blame or guilt

        1. "I'm sorry this bill is so upsetting to you."

        2. "I'm sorry you thought this was a covered service."

    B. Verify the facts
       "Let me see if I understand what happened . . ."

    C. Explain what you can do; provide general overview of the process you will follow to resolve the concern
       "I'd be happy to help you. Let me check into this and get back to you with the information I learn."

    D. Agree on next contact
       "I'm going to look into this for you and get back to you [time frame]"—hopefully in 24 hours/up to 48 hours

III. Problem Solve

    A. Consult with others

        1. Exchange information: patient received bill because

           a. Coverage not effective on the date of service

           b. Medical condition determined to be a noncovered service

           c. Service was not included in the referral

        2. Review records—is the documentation complete enough for a HCFA review?

    B. Explore and identify options

        1. If charges are appropriate, can payment arrangements be made?

        2. Is the dollar amount worth the expense of appealing to HCFA?

    C. Update consumer if necessary

IV. Respond/Refer
    Contact patient/customer with customized resolution

        1. "I learned that you received a bill for those services because _____. The information that these services aren't covered is in the Certificate of Coverage you received when you enrolled in the Madrona Medigap program."

        2. "I learned that you received a bill for those services because _____. The referral from Dr. Jones specified we treat you only for [condition]."

V. Follow-Up

    A. Bring closure to complaint — summarize patient/customer's request, the actions you took, and agreed-upon resolution

        1. "Even though this was not a service covered by Medicare, we have made a one-time-only decision to write-off these charges as a good-faith gesture."

2. "We will be appealing Madrona Medigap's decision to not cover those appointments you had with the nurse. It may take some time, so we will put a hold on your account until the appeal is completed."

B. Thank patient/customer

1. "Thank you for calling us, and I'm sorry this was confusing to sort out. I appreciate your patience while we researched your coverage."

2. "Thank you for calling us, and I'm sorry we weren't able to help you."

C. Share your organization's Service Recovery standards, if appropriate

1. You strive to recognize the patient/customer as an individual

2. You strive to provide the patient/customer with an easy, obvious process for sharing concerns

3. You strive to provide the patient/customer with a key contact person

4. You strive for a fair resolution

5. You strive for a fast resolution

6. You strive to provide consistent, clear, and accurate information

D. Written follow-up letter

1. Summarize patient/customer's request, the actions you took, and agreed-upon resolution

2. Apologize for the patient/customer's feelings of dissatisfaction or inconvenience

3. Report any system changes that have occurred as a result of this complaint

4. Offer to assist in the future if needed

E. Document complaint and distribute, if appropriate

▼ Home Health Agency Staff
Multiple Providers

I. Patient/Customer Contact

A. Listen—focus on the patient/customer with attentive body language (if in person) and voice inflections (if over the telephone)

B. Ask open-ended questions

1. "How many RN [aides] have you seen?"

2. "Can you tell me a little more about your concern?"

C. Empathize; validate the patient/customer's perspective
"I understand how frustrated you are."

D. Clarify the patient/customer's expectation for resolution

II. Acknowledge

    A. Apologize—without assigning blame or guilt
"I'm sorry this isn't what you were expecting."

    B. Verify the facts
"Let me make sure I understand what you've told me."

    C. Explain what you can do; provide general overview of the process you will follow to resolve the concern
"I understand that you do not want to be seen by so many different people. I will document your concern and share it with Ms. Smith, our clinical care supervisor. She is the person who reviews all the schedules."

    D. Agree on next contact
"I'm going to ask Ms. Smith to call you [time frame]"—hopefully in 24 hours/up to 48 hours

III. Respond/Refer

    A. Transfer complaint to appropriate supervisor

        1. Contact the supervisor and relay all the pertinent information and facts about the problem

        2. Negotiate with the supervisor to assume responsibility for investigating, reviewing, and/or resolving the problem; determine who will notify the patient/customer with the final resolution

        3. Document in writing the pertinent facts and the plan for resolution, and send a copy to the supervisor

IV. Follow-Up

    A. Bring closure to complaint
Summarize patient/customer's request, the actions you took, and agreed-upon resolution

    B. Thank patient/customer
"Thank you for sharing this concern with me. We want you to be satisfied with the service you receive from us."

    C. Share your organization's Service Recovery standards, if appropriate

        1. You strive to recognize the patient/customer as an individual

        2. You strive to provide the patient/customer with an easy, obvious process for sharing concerns

        3. You strive to provide the patient/customer with a key contact person

        4. You strive for a fair resolution

        5. You strive for a fast resolution

        6. You strive to provide consistent, clear, and accurate information

Appendix F

Procedure for Formal Medical Staff Review of Quality-of-Care Complaints

▼ **Procedures for Review**

Procedure	Time Frame
1. Patient contacts Patient Representative and is mailed complaint form for signature, and medical records release form if non-Plan care was received.	Sent within one working day
2. a. If patient does not respond, a letter is sent, encouraging patient to follow up with concern. b. If non-Plan care is involved, and records have not arrived, a letter is sent advising the patient to follow up with the provider. c. Patient returns signed complaint form; acknowledgement letter is sent to patient.	Written within 15 working days Written within 15 days after Patient Representative receives signed complaint form from patient Written within one working day

205

▼ Procedures for Review *(continued)*

Procedure	Time Frame
3. Packet of information is compiled containing applicable medical records, the patient's letter, and any other appropriate information.	Sent within two working days of receiving all necessary information
a. Follow-up letter is sent to patient advising that review has been initiated and will take two to three weeks to complete.	Written within one working day
b. Medical Staff providers involved in complaint are sent a packet by Patient Representative, and asked to review the contents and report their findings to the Chief of Staff.	Respond within five working days of receiving packet
c. The Chief of Staff is sent packet and asked to review the contents and responses, and report his findings to the Patient Representative. If non-Medical Staff providers (i.e., RNs, MAs, or other providers who do not report to the Medical Staff) are involved in the complaint, the Chief of Staff's office will contact the appropriate supervisor and the provider directly for their comments.	Respond within eight working days of receiving packet
4. Patient Representative writes a draft letter advising the patient of the results of the review, and sends it to Chief of Staff for approval.	Written within two working days of receiving the Chief of Staff's response
5. Patient Representative sends letter to patient, advising of the results of the review.	Sent within one working day of receiving comments from Chief of Staff regarding draft

▼ Contents of Level 5 and Level 6 Medical Staff Review Packet

I. Packet for providers involved in care of patient for this condition

   A. *Cover memo with request for written response to Chief of Staff's office in five working days.* Memo is cc:'d to Chief of Staff, physician's facility/section chief (for information), physician's facility manager (for information), and, if applicable, provider's preceptor (for information).

   B. *Copy of patient's written complaint*

   C. *Copy of patient's medical records* that are relevant to the complaint in chronological order

   D. *Copy of non-Plan medical records,* if applicable

II. *Packet for Chief of Staff*

    A. *Cover memo with request for response to Patient Representative in eight working days.* If financial settlement is requested, state the amount.

    B. *Copy of patient's written complaint*

    C. *Copy of patient's medical records* that are relevant to the complaint in chronological order

    D. *Copy of non-Plan medical records,* if applicable

    E. *Anything else that may help Chief of Staff with review*

III. *Packet for Physician's Facility/Section Chief; Physician's Facility Manager; Provider's Preceptor*

    A. *Copy of cover memo to physician*

    B. *Copy of patient's written complaint*

All packets should be sealed in an envelope marked:
> **"CONFIDENTIAL—OPEN BY ADDRESSEE ONLY"**

All copies of patient's written complaint and cover memos should be clearly marked:
"CONFIDENTIAL INFORMATION—DO NOT FILE IN PATIENT'S CHART."

▼ Final Letters in Level 5 and Level 6 Quality-of-Care Cases

1. Chief of Staff discusses results of review with Patient Representative

2. Within two working days, Patient Representative sends draft of final letter to Chief of Staff for comment

3. Patient Representative incorporates any of the Chief of Staff's recommended changes to the letter and mails it to the patient

4. The letter is distributed as follows

    a. the original is sent to the patient

    b. the letter is cc:'d to the Chief of Staff's office

    c. the letter is bcc:'d (blind copied) to the providers involved in reviewing the complaint

    d. a copy is filed in the formal case folder

▼ Guidelines for Referring Cases to Risk Management

The following are brief guidelines for the relationship between the Patient Representative and Risk Management.

I. Basis for direct referral of a patient complaint to Risk Management
   A. Patient has stated he is dissatisfied with the care provided, directly or indirectly asserting "negligent care," and is seeking
      1. Compensation for the alleged pain and suffering related to the care
      2. **and** Payment of bills for care received at another facility
      3. **or** Arrangement for special additional treatment to resolve the problem at no charge
      4. **or** Patient is threatening to sue or states an attorney has been contacted
   B. Patient has retained representation of an attorney to handle the claim and request for general compensation

II. Basis for advising Risk Management for possible consultation or involvement in the handling of a patient complaint:*
   A. Patient is requesting consideration for a significant amount of bills (i.e., over $5,000) in relation to quality-of-care issues
   B. Patient is unhappy or dissatisfied with Plan physician's opinion, and is pressing to seek a second opinion at a non-Plan facility with the Plan covering the associated costs
   C. Concern exists regarding patient's level of dissatisfaction with medical care, the significance of the resultant damages claimed, and an indication by the patient that future legal action is under consideration

   *In most of these cases, the Patient Representative will continue to review the complaint following normal procedures. If the case continues to escalate, referral to Risk Management will need to be reconsidered.

▼ Case Files

Proper documentation of cases is important to the credibility of the complaint-resolution program. Consistency and order in the filing of complaints enhances the retrievability of additional information later, and in reviewing the process. Below is the description of a system for organizing case packets in a logical sequence.

Contents of Level 5 and Level 6 Case Files*

I. Left side

    A. Patient Representative's completed Report Form

    B. Patient's written complaint

    C. Copy of final letter to patient

    D. Progress notes

    E. Correspondence with patient (chronological order)

    F. Memos (copies) to physicians, administrators etc.

II. Right side

    A. Copies of all bills, with summary sheet and total

    B. Copies of patient's medical records applicable to complaint

    C. Non-Plan records if applicable

    D. Other pertinent information (e.g., articles, copies of policies etc.)

    * Assumes case is filed in folder with pockets on each side.

▼ Contents of Level 1 through Level 4 Case Files

1. Completed Report Form—required for *all* Patient Representative cases

2. Letter from patient (if complaint was written)

3. Letter from Patient Representative (if letter was written in response, rather than when contacting patient by telephone)

4. Progress notes

5. Applicable medical records

6. Bills or other pertinent information

Appendix G

Subjects of Complaints

Patients will report complaints about a variety of issues. The following lists of topics and subcategories of those topics are ideas that can be modified to meet the needs of different facilities or organizations. The subcategories are stated from the patient's perspective.

Sometimes staff have difficulty determining whether the problem the patient brings is a request for assistance or a complaint. They can also have difficulty deciding the subject of the complaint.

The following diagram, Figure G-1, is intended to help staff through this decision process.

Figure G-1 Subject Decision Diagram

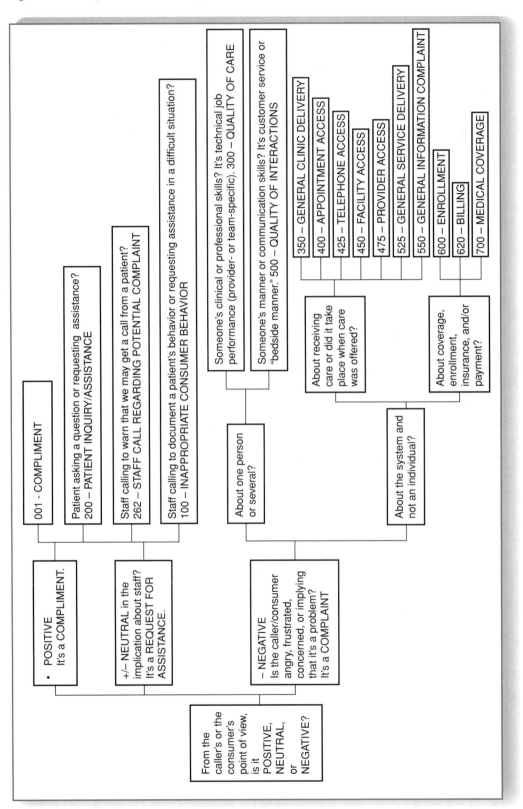

Once staff have chosen the subject of the complaint, they can use the following list to more specifically identify the complaint or inquiry. This list is intended as an example, or starting point, for developing a list applicable for the particular facility or organization.

Inquiry

200 General Assistance (used when others are not applicable)

Orientation

201 General orientation (used when others are not applicable)

202 Choosing a clinic (new patient)

203 Changing a clinic

204 Choosing a physician (new patient)

205 Changing physicians

Access to Service

210 General access to service (used when others are not applicable)

211 Providing directions to facilities

212 Providing phone numbers

213 Making an appointment

Assistance with Medical Care

220 General assistance with medical care (used when others are not applicable)

221 Problem solving regarding follow-up care

222 Second opinion process

Clarification of Policy/Procedure

230 General questions about policies/procedures (used when others are not applicable)

231 Obtaining copy of medical records

233 Advanced Directives

Billing/Enrollment

240 General billing/enrollment questions (used when others are not applicable)

241 Clarification of billing

242 Clarification of coverage

243 Processing bill for payment

244 Changing coverage

245   Requests fee quote for noncovered service

246   Financial assistance (uncompensated care)

Miscellaneous Inquiries

250   Finding lost articles

251   Patient suggestion for improved services

Quality of Medical Care

Provider-Specific Concerns

300   General concerns about medical care (used when others are not applicable

301   Superficial/incomplete exam, history taking, diagnostic work-up/not enough tests

302   Disagrees with diagnosis

303   Disagrees with treatment

304   Disagrees with diagnosis and treatment

305   Provider's technical skill (casting, blood draw, painful mammogram, etc.)

306   Treatment not aggressive enough/not progressing fast enough

307   Referral for specialty services denied, delayed, or not urgent enough

308   Lack of information regarding treatment plan, prognosis, need for follow-up care

309   Discharged from the hospital too soon (physically not ready for discharge)

310   Hospitalization denied or not offered

311   Physician refuses to authorize or refill Rx

312   Denied appointment via telephone triage

313   Error in chart documentation

314   Coordination of care

315   Family/friend/employer disagrees with physician's diagnosis or treatment

316   Infection-control protocols not followed (not wearing gloves, did not wash hands)

Delivery System Concerns That Impact Clinical Care

350   General concerns about delivery system (used when others are not applicable)

351   Continuity of care (seen by multiple providers, can't access own primary care physician)

352   Complete medical record not available for appointment

353   Appointment time too brief

354   Communication of test results (timing, content)

355   Pharmacy dispensing error

Quality of Service

Access to Services

Appointment Access

400   General appointment access issues (used when others are not applicable)

401   Well child/routine physical/annual exam delay

402   Routine appointment delay

403   Follow-up appointment delay

404   Urgent/emergent appointment delay

405   Nonelective surgery delay

406   Elective surgery delay

407   "Get acquainted visit" availability

408   Appointment books not open

409   Reschedule—patient canceled, did not appear, or late

410   Reschedule—staff cancel, inclement weather

411   Referral process internal/external (paperwork delayed, lost, etc.)

412   Scheduling error by staff

413   Appointment-making process (flexibility, number of appointments, ease of appointment making)

414   Department closed when should be open

415   Lack of drop-in care

416   Facility hours (evenings, lunch coverage, etc.)

Telephone Access

425   General telephone access issues (used when others are not applicable)

426   Long distance phone issues (lack of "800" numbers, etc.)

427   Problems while on hold (including disconnects)

428   Lines busy

429   Busy signals *and* problems while on hold

430   Phone rings, no answer

431   Lack of direct phone access to RN or MD

432   Not called back in a timely manner

433   Use of telephone recorder, sequencer, voice-mail system

434   Telephone triage process

Facility Access

450   General facility access issues (used when others are not applicable)

451   Travel time/transportation to and from facility

452   Parking

453   Lack of disabled parking

454   Construction

455   Wheelchair access

456   Urgent care services located in unsafe neighborhood

457   Hospital admit night before surgery

Provider Access

475   General concerns about provider access (used when others are not applicable)

476   Physician of preferred gender, race, philosophy of care not available

477   Access to specific closed practice

478   Primary care physician availability (no, or few, open practices)

479   Utilization of mid-level practitioners

480   Split practice (practice shared by two part-time physicians)

481   Licensed practitioners

482   Unable to self-refer to specialty services

483   Specialty service not available locally

Staff Attitude (or Customer Service Orientation)

500   General attitude (used when others not applicable)

501   Lack of courtesy/rude/unhelpful

502   Condescending/scolding/accusing/paternalistic

503   Inappropriate physical contact

504   Doesn't take patient seriously

505   Unprofessional appearance

506   Personal business delays staff response or treatment of patient

507   Lack of response when service or information is requested

508   Refused or denied requested service

509   Lack of personalized care or lack of attentiveness to patient needs

510   Preservation of dignity

511	Confidentiality breached
512	Discrimination
513	Brushes patient off/cold/uninterested/unhelpful/abrupt
514	Unprofessional/inappropriate comments
515	Insensitive to feelings
516	Insensitive to ethnic/cultural/socioeconomic status/age/gender

Service Delivery

525	General service delivery issues (used when others are not applicable)
526	Check-in/registration/admitting procedures
527	Waiting room delay
528	Exam room delay
529	Service delay (dispensing Rx, wait for lab test, etc.)
530	Delay of scheduled tests or procedures within the hospital
531	Equipment/building/furniture/plants
532	Noise
533	Cleanliness
534	Food—inpatient or cafeteria
535	Lack of privacy in consultation
536	No chaperone present during examination
537	Loss or theft of property (dentures, glasses, jewelry, etc.)
538	Hospital discharge does not go smoothly
539	Dispensing, return, release of Rx practices (pharmacy, optical)
540	Timely form completion (L&I, personal insurance, return-to-work forms, etc.)

Information

550	General concerns about information issues (use when others are not applicable)
551	lack of information regarding tests or procedures
552	Misinformation or lack of complete information regarding coverage or change in coverage benefits
553	Misinformation or lack of complete information regarding policies or services
554	Requests for improved new enrollee orientation
555	Lack of notification when physician leaves

556   Lack of notification of facility changes (phone numbers, department move, changes in staffing patterns)

557   Interpretive services

Financial/Enrollment

600   General financial or enrollment issues (used when others are not applicable)

601   Enrollment status dispute (includes new enrollees not yet entered on enrollee database)

602   Incorrect personal data on enrollee database (wrong address, misspelled name)

603   Problem with identification card requests

604   Enrollment terminated without notice

605   Timely refund or reimbursement

606   Timely premium billing

607   Timely processing of payments made at clinics

608   Timely reactivation of inactive enrollment

609   Dependent eligibility letter

610   Timely or accurate processing of non-Plan billings

611   Non-Plan referral paperwork delayed or inaccurate

612   Disputed billing (billed incorrectly or in error)

613   Incorrect fee quotes

614   Cashier error, incorrect change

615   Check posted to incorrect account

616   Collection process

617   Benefit limit tracking system

Policy

Medical Coverage Benefits/Policies

700   General coverage policy (used when others are not applicable)

701   Plastic/cosmetic surgery

702   Sterilization

703   Contraception

704   Abortion

705   Infertility/impotency/sex change/frigidity

706   Amniocentesis

707   Mental health—inpatient benefit ($ limit)

708   Mental health—outpatient benefit ($ or visit limit)

709   Excluded mental health treatment (e.g., long-term, court-ordered, etc.)

710   Alcohol/drugs—inpatient

711   Alcohol/drugs—outpatient

712   Experimental/investigational treatment

713   Chiropractic services

714   Podiatry services

715   Other licensed practitioner services

716   Orthopedic appliances

717   Coverage for prosthetics

718   Durable medical equipment or supplies (wheelchair, diabetic, or ostomy supplies)

719   Contact lenses

720   Glasses (optical benefit)

721   Prescription drugs/immunizations (nonformulary, travel)

722   Over-the-counter medications

723   Pharmacy charges (mailing, replacement Rx, etc.)

724   Reciprocity

725   Emergency benefit (deductible, nonemergent treatment)

726   Emergency benefit (unauthorized follow-up care)

727   Ambulance benefit (deductible, nonemergency, benefit limit, no preauthorization)

728   Emergency Room co-pay

729   Emergency admission to non-Plan hospital, Plan not notified

730   Emergency admit to another hospital—refuses transfer to Plan hospital

731   Emergency Room bills denied because area clinic open

732   Expired referral/services not included in referral

733   Permanent surgical waivers for preexisting condition

734   Obesity/eating disorders treatment

735   Sleep apnea

736   Fees (form completion, personal insurance, Rx mailing, etc.)

737   Co-pays

738   Oral surgery/TMJ/dental treatment

739   Rehab/therapy (PT, OT, ST) limits or exclusions

740   Early discharge/decertification (patient physically ready for discharge but patient/family believes no acceptable place to go)

741   Charges too high

742   Co-pays for preventive care services

743   Lock-in

744   Deductibles

745   Subrogation/third party/COB

746   Care received prior to or after effective date of coverage

747   Coverage for unauthorized non-Plan care or services (after the fact)

748   Requests referral for non-Plan services

749   Skilled nursing care

750   Long-term nursing home care

751   Home health/hospice care

Operational Policies

800   General operations policies (used when others are not applicable)

801   Enrollment eligibility

802   Dependent coverage eligibility

803   Termination of coverage

804   Reinstatement of coverage

805   Private patient policy (will only see enrollees)

806   Age rating

807   Advertising/promotional activities

808   Changes in staffing ratios (RNs/MAs/LPNs/etc.)

809   Drug testing policies/procedures

810   No smoking policy

811   Political action/endorsement of legislation by the Plan

812   Custodial parent vs. contract holder receiving insurance coverage information

813   Access to records

814   Confidentiality of records

815   Records provided only with written authorization to third party

816   Informed consent

817   Modification of medical record or deletion of information

818   Privacy for minors per state law (alcohol/drug treatment, pregnancy, contraception, etc.)

819   Authorization of treatment of children

820   Family objects to lack of access to patient's records

821   Hospital visiting policy

822   Parent staying with child in hospital

823   Child/Adult Protective Services reporting

Complaint Handling

150   General dissatisfaction with complaint handling (used when others are not applicable)

151   Complaint handler not helpful or discourteous

152   Resolution not timely

153   Resolution not acceptable

Abusive Patient Behavior

100   General inappropriate patient behavior (used when others are not applicable)

101   Verbal abuse/harassment

102   Threat of physical contact

103   Nonconsensual physical contact

104   Assault (fear of immediate harm)

105   Did not appear for appointment

106   Misuse of services (use of ER for routine care, etc.)

107   Noncompliance with organization policies (no smoking, timely payment of bills/premiums)

108   Misuse/abuse of patient identification card

109   Alteration or forgery of prescription; theft of prescription forms

110   Noncompliance with treatment plan (MD no longer wants to follow patient)

111   Theft of or damage to property

112   Drug-seeking behavior

Additional Readings

Albrecht, K., and R. Zemke. *Service America! Doing Business in the New Economy.* Homewood, IL: Dow Jones-Irwin, 1985.

American Hospital Association. *Healthcare Patient Advocate Job Related Member Survey.* Chicago: AHA, 1997.

American Hospital Association. *Managing Violence in the Healthcare Arena.* Chicago: AHA, audiotape.

Anderson, K., and R. Zemke. *Delivering Knock Your Socks Off Service.* New York: AMACOM Books, 1991.

Anderson, K. and R. Zemke. *Knock Your Socks Off Answers: Solving Customer Nightmares and Soothing Nightmare Customers.* New York: AMACOM Books, 1995.

Barlow, J. and C. Moller. *A Complaint Is a Gift.* San Francisco: Berrett-Koehler, 1996.

Baum, N., and L. Osborne. *Correspondence for the Clinical Practice.* Columbus: Anadem Publishing, 1996.

Becker, H. *At Your Service: Calamities, Catastrophes, and Other Curiosities of Customer Service.* New York: John Wiley and Sons, 1998.

Bell, C.R. "Customer Candor: A Tool for Partnerships." *Mobius* (Spring 1990).

Bell, C.R., and F.C. Sims. "Casting Customer Service People." *Supervisory Management* (June 1990).

Bell, C.R., and R. Zemke. "Do Service Procedures Tie Employee Hands?" *Personnel Journal* (September 1988).

Bell, C.R., and R. Zemke. "Service Breakdown: The Road to Recovery." *Management Review* (October 1987).

Berry, L.L. *On Great Service: A Framework for Action.* New York: The Free Press, 1995.

Berry, L.L., and A. Parasuraman. *Marketing Services: Competing Through Quality.* New York: The Free Press, 1991.

Brown, S.W., A. Nelson, S.J. Bronkesh, and S.D. Wood. *Patient Satisfaction Pays: Quality Service for Practice Success.* Gaithersburg, MD: Aspen Publishers, Inc, 1993.

Center for Disease Control and National Institute for Occupational Safety and Health. *Violence: Occupational Hazards in Hospitals.* Publication No. 2002-101 (April 2002).

Connellan, T.K., and R. Zemke. *Sustaining Knock Your Socks Off Service.* New York: AMACOM Books, 1993.

Crosby, P.B. *Quality Is Free: The Art of Making Quality Certain.* New York: McGraw-Hill Book Company, 1979.

Crosby, P.B. *Quality Without Tears: The Art of Hassle-Free Management.* New York: New American Library, 1984.

Desatnick, R.L. *Managing to Keep the Customer: How to Achieve and Maintain Superior Customer Service Throughout the Organization.* San Francisco: Jossey-Bass Publishers, 1987.

Friedman, N. *Customer Service Nightmares.* Menlo Park, CA: Crisp Publications, 1998.

Gilbert, J., and H. Harrison. *The Written Word: Guidelines for Responding in Writing to Patient Concerns.* Chicago: AHA, 2002.

Goodman, J.A. "The Nature of Customer Satisfaction." Paper presented at the National Quality Forum IV, New York: 1988 (revised 1993).

Goodman, J.A., and C.J. Grimm. "A Quantified Case for Improving Quality Now!" *Journal for Quality and Participation* (March 1990), pp. 50–55.

Goodman, J.A., A.R. Malech, G.F. Bargatze, and C. Ledbetter. "Converting a Desire for Quality Service into Actions with Measurable Impact." *Journal of Retail Banking* (Winter 1988–1989), pp.14–22.

Goodman, J.A., and A.R. Malech. "Don't Fix the Product, Fix the Customer." *The Quality Review* (Fall 1988), pp. 6–11.

Goodman, J. "Basic Facts on Customer Complaint Behavior and the Impact of Service on the Bottom Line." *Competitive Advantage.* <www.e-Satisfy.com>, pp. 1–5.

Grimme, S., and D. Grimme. "Violence in the Workplace: The Realties and the Options." <www.businessknowhow.com/manage/violwork.htm>; <www.GHR-Training.com>.

Krowinski, W. J., S. R. Steiber. *Measuring and Managing Patient Satisfaction.* San Francisco: Jossey-Bass Publishers, (September 1996).

Leebov, W. *Service Excellence: The Customer Relations Strategy for Health Care.* Chicago: American Hospital Publishing, 1988.

Levitt, T. "After the Sale is Over." Harvard Business Review (September–October, 1983).

Morgan, R.L. *Calming Upset Customers.* Menlo Park, CA: Crisp Publications, 1996.

Schaaf, R., and R. Zemke. *Taking Care of Business: 101 Ways to Keep Them Coming Back.* Minneapolis: Lakewood Books, 1991.

Society for Healthcare Consumer Advocacy. *In the Name of the Patient.* Chicago: AHA, 2002.

Technical Assistance Research Programs (TARP). *Increasing Customer Satisfaction Through Effective Corporate Complaint Handling.* U.S. Office of Consumer Affairs, Consumer Information Center, Dept. 606R, Pueblo, CO, 81009.

Technical Assistance Research Programs (TARP). *Using Complaints for Quality Assurance Decisions* (1997). <www.e-Satisfy.com>.

U.S. Department of Health and Human Services, Public Health Service, Center for Disease Control and Prevention, National Institute for Occupational Safety and Health. Violence in the Workplace. Current Intelligence. Bulletin 57 (July 1996). <www.cdc.gov/niosh/violdev/html>.

Zeithaml, V.A., A. Parasuraman, and L.L. Berry. *Delivering Quality Service: Balancing Customer Perceptions and Expectations.* New York: The Free Press, 1990.

Zemke, R., and C.R. Bell. *Service Wisdom.* Minneapolis, MN.: Lakewood Books, 1990.

Zemke, R., and C.R. Bell. "Service Recovery: Doing It Right the Second Time." *Training* (June 1990).

Zemke, R. *The Service Edge: 101 Companies That Profit From Customer Care.* New York: New American Library, 1989.

Index

A

Abusive patient behavior. *See* Patients, difficult
Accountability, physician, 85
Administrators, benefits, 2
Anderson, Kristen, 22
Annoyed customer, 23–24
Apologies, 15, 65
Appointments
    access to, 123–127, 215
    missed, 100–101
Atonement, 18
Attitude, staff
    categories for, 216–217
    protocols for, 127–129, 154–156, 172–174

B

Bain and company, 5
Bayne, Ken, 106
Behavior, unacceptable. *See* Patients, difficult
Bell, Chip, 9
Benefits administrators, 2
Berry, Leonard, *Delivering Quality Service: Balancing Customer Perceptions and Expectations*, 3–4
Billing complaints
    categories for, 213–214, 218, 219, 220
    credits for, 81
    letters regarding, 56-59

protocols for, 81
    write-offs for, 81–82
Billing, for services from others providers, 82
Blame, 6. *See also* Culpability scale
Blasé blue complaints, 22–23, 24, 25, 27
    letters regarding, 62–63
    review of, 32–34
    time to resolution, 77–78
Body language, 14–15

C

CAL/OSHA, 116
Case files, contents of, 39–41, 208-209
Case manager, 77
Case report form, 32, 72–76, 87
    distribution of, 82
    sample forms, 73, 76
Center for Disease Control (CDC), 116
Chavez, Larry J., 97
Chief of staff
    memo, regarding review of complaints, 40
    role of, 90
        in formal quality of care review, 39
        in physician complaints, 85, 86, 87
Clinical review process. *See* Quality of care complaints, review
Closure, to problem-solving process, 17–18
Coding. *See* Complaints, categories; tracking

Communication, with patient, 14–16, 17–18. *See also* Letters, to patient and avoiding litigation, 30
Complainants, 78
Complaint form, sample, 36
Complaints
    acknowledging, 15–16
    bringing to closure, 16–18
    categories
        diagram for, 212
        list of, 213–221
    criteria for handling, 6–7
    documentation. *See* Documentation, of complaints
    formal review of, 34–43
    frequent vs. important, 10, 11
    informal review of, 32, 34
    as isolated incident, 96–97
    letters regarding, 65
    levels of complexity, 25–27
    non-physician, trends in, 92
    physician, 85–89
    quality of care. *See* Quality of care
    quality of service. *See* Quality of service
    referring to others, 16–17, 34–35
    regarding policy, 65, 79–80
    tracking, 10, 11, 72, 77–82
    value of, 11, 71
    written, 35–36
Compliment/complaint profile, form, 86
Concern, soliciting, 14–15
Conditions of participation, Medicare/Medicaid, 29–30
Confidentiality, 39, 78, 78–79
Contact, customer, 14–15
    and "moments of truth", 3
Correspondence, with patients. *See* Letters, to patient
Cost containment, 2, 5–6, 7
CQI (continuous quality management), 2, 5, 11, 71
Crosby, Philip, 2
Culpability scale, 21–22
Customer. *See also* Patient
    annoyed, 23–24. *See also* Ornery orange complaints
    contact, 3, 14–15
    expectations of, 13
    loyalty. *See* Loyalty, customer
    retaining vs. replacing, 5–6, 7
    turnover, rate of, 5–6
    victimized, 23–24. *See also* Red hot complaints

Customer service nightmares, 3, 10
Customer Service Nightmares (Friedman), 3

D
Decertification, notification of, 60–61
Decision zones. *See* Solution spaces
Delivering Knock Your Socks Off Service (Anderson and Zemke), 22–23
Delivering Quality Service (Berry, Parasuraman and Zeithaml), 3–4
Deming, W. Edwards, 2
Documentation, 17, 18. *See also* Letters
    of abusive patient behavior, 80
    of patient complaints, 31–32, 35–43, 71-76, 82-83
    of quality of care cases, 207
    of service recovery activities, 25, 26, 30
    of workplace violence, 118–119
DOGS (defusing of grievance = safety), 97
Drug seeking patients, 99–100, 104–106

E
Emergency room "frequent fliers", 99
Emotional overlay, 7, 21, 22–24
Employees. *See* Staff
Expectations, of patient, 1–2, 2–3, 13
    role in review process, 27, 30

F
Facilities, appearance of, 4
Family
    as complainant, 78
    overly involved, 95–96
Financial damages, 34–35, 37
    settlement of, letters regarding, 68–70
Forms
    case report, 71–82
    compliment/complaint profile, physician, 86
Frequent fliers, emergency room, 99
Friedman, Nancy, *Customer Service Nightmares*, 3

G
Gallup poll, on workplace violence, 116
Gender, of complainant, 78
Goodman, J. A., 6
Grievance process, HCFA, 29–30
Grimme, Don and Sheryl, 97, 106
Guest relations, 2

H
HCFA (Health Care Financing Administration), 29–30

Head injured patients, 96
Home health agencies, protocols for, 195–203
    clinician late for appointment, 197–199
    disputed billing, 200–202
    model, 195–197
    multiple providers, 202–203
    quality of care, 199–200

I
Inquiries, patient, categories for, 213–214
Insurance benefits administrators, 2
Interpersonal skills, of physician, 88–89

K
Kubinski, Ronald, 9

L
Law-breaking patients, 102–106
Letters
    to other facilities
        regarding bills and medical records,
            56–57
        requesting hold or suspension of billing,
            58–59
    to patient, 47–55, 60–70
        complaint form only, 47
        follow-up, 18, 50–51
        initial, 45–48
        progress report, 52–55
        regarding bills and medical records, 49
        regarding decertification, 60–61
        regarding identity misrepresentation,
            103
        regarding missed appointments, 101
        regarding prescription fraud, 105
        regarding quality of care, 207
        regarding results of review, 62–66
        regarding transfer of case to risk
            management, 66–67
        regarding verbal abuse, 107–111
    to physicians, regarding program participaton,
        90–92
Levels, of complaint complexity
    1–4, 25–26, 32–34
        contents of case files, 208–209
        resolving, 78
        time to resolution, 77–78
    5–6, 26–27
        contents of case files, 39–41, 208–209
        resolving, 78
        time to resolution, 78
    documentation of, 78

Litigation, avoiding, 7, 29–30
Loyalty, customer, 5, 5–6, 7
    identifying problems involving, 9–12
Loyalty factors, 10

M
Malpractice litigation, 30
Marketing department/business office, protocols
    for, 167–193
    appointment wait time, 169–172
    billing disputes, 174–178
    enrollment status dispute, 186–188
    incorrect personal data, 178–180
    insurance card request, 180–183
    lack of information about coverage, 183–186
    model, 167–169
    referral process, 189–190
Medical College of Wisconsin, 30
Medical director. *See* Chief of staff
Medical model, vs. service recovery model, 13
Medical records
    and identity theft, 102
    release of, 37
Medical staff review, procedures for, 205–207.
    See also Quality of care complaints,
    review
Medicare, decertification, 60–61
Medicare, Medicaid, conditions for participation,
    29–30
Member services department. *See* Marketing
    department/business office
Memos
    to chief of staff reviewing complaints, 38
    to individual physician, 33
    to providers reviewing complaints, 38
Moment of truth, 3, 4

N
National Institute for Occupational Safety,
    CDC, 116
Noncompliant patients, 96
Nonverbal communication, 14–15
Nursing staff, 31–32, 116

O
Office of Consumer Affairs, U. S., 6
Ornery orange complaints, 23, 25–26, 27
    letters regarding, 62–63
    review of, 32–34
    time to resolution, 77–78
OSHA, and workplace violence, 116–117
Overutilization of services, 98–99

P

Parasuraman, A., *Delivering Quality Service: Balancing Customer Perceptions and Expectations*, 3–4
Patient
　communication with, 30
　rights of, 29–30
　turnover rate, 5–6
Patient complaint form, sample, 36
Patient inquiries, categories for, 213–214
Patient loyalty. *See* Loyalty, customer
Patient-physician relationship, 1–2, 6, 7, 88–89
　and malpractice litigation, 30
Patient representative department, protocols
　　for, 149–166
　access to MD, 161–163
　appointment wait time, 151–154
　denial of services, 158–161
　handling complaints, 156–158
　model, 149–151
　quality of care, 163–166
　staff attitude, 154–156
Patient representatives, role of, 39, 42
　with patient, 78
　with physician, 87, 88
　reducing litigation, 30, 31
　and risk managers, 34–35
Patient-staff relationship, 10–11
Patients. *See also* Customers
Patients, difficult
　abusive
　　categories for, 221
　　five factors of, 106–107
　　physically threatening, 116–119
　　and sexual harassment, 112–113
　　verbally, 107–111, 114–115
　annoying, 94
　drug seekers, 99–100
　head injury, 95
　historians, 94–95
　know-it-alls, 107
　and missed appointments, 100
　noncompliant, 96
　and overly involved family, 95–96
　overutilizers of service, 98–99
　socially isolated, 95
　system abusers, 97–100
Patients, lawbreaking
　identity misrepresentation, 102–104
　prescription forgery, 104–106
Performance Research Associates, Inc., 9, 21
Physician-patient relationship, 1–2, 6, 7, 88–89

and malpractice litigation, 30
Physicians
　access to, 129–133, 145–146, 161–163
　clinical review process, 31, 32–34
　interpersonal skills of, 88–89
　protocols for
　　access, 141–148
　　quality of care, 144–145
　　waiting room delay, 143–144
　status of, 1–2
Policy
　complaints regarding, 65, 79–80
　　categories, 218–221
　on workplace violence, 117–118
Problems. *See also* Complaints
　developing options to resolve, 11–12
　identifying frequent, 10–11
　system, 11–12, 89
　tracking, 10, 11
Protocols
　developing, 9–12, 23–24
　for home health agencies. *See* Home health
　　agencies, protocols for
　for member services department. *See*
　　Marketing department/business office,
　　protocols for
　for patient representative department. *See*
　　Patient representative department,
　　protocols for
　for physicians. *See* Physicians, protocols for

Q

Quality assurance (QA), 71, 77
Quality of care complaints, 80
　categories for, 214–215
　letters regarding, 62–66, 207
　protocols for, 134–136, 144–145, 163–166,
　　199–200
　review of, 29–43
　　formal, 34–43, 205–207
　　against medical staff, 32–34
　　memos regarding, 33, 38, 40
　　against nursing and ancillary staff, 31–
　　　32
　　patient response to, 43
Quality of service
　complaints regarding, 80. *See also* Staff
　　attitude
　　categories for, 215–218
　components of, 80
　evaluation of, 3–4
Quick form, 11

R

Receptionists, medical, protocols for, 121–139
  and access to physician, 129–133
  and pharmacy wait, 133–134
  and phone access, 137–138
  and quality of care, 134–136
  and return call from RN, 136–137
  and scheduling appointment, 123–127
  and staff attitude, 127–129
  and waiting room delay, 138–139
Red hot complaints, 23, 26–27
  letters regarding, 64–67
  review of, 34–43
  time to resolution, 78
Release of information, 78
Reputation, facility, 4
Retaining customers, 5–6, 7
Review of complaint, depth of, 25–27
Review process, for quality of care complaints.
      See Quality of care complaints, review
Rights, of patient, 29–30
Risk Management, 7, 90
  criteria for involving, 34–35
  as customers, 71
  involvement of, 26, 30, 31
  and patient representatives, 34–35
  referring case to, guidelines, 208
  traditional approach of, 29
  transferring case to, letters regarding, 66–67

S

Satisfaction, patient, 29, 83
Service
  components of, 80
  criteria for evaluating, 3–4
  intangible nature of, 2
  recognition of outstanding, 92
Service recovery
  definition, 5
  establishing protocols for, 10–12, 23–24
  importance of, 5–6, 7–8
  model, vs. medical model, 13
  six steps of, 14–18
    acknowledge the problem, 15–16
    atonement, 18
    customer contact, 14–15
    follow up, 17–18

  problem solve and respond, 16
  refer/respond, 16–17
Sexual harassment, 112–113, 116
Shapiro, R. S., 30
Solution spaces, 12–13
  implementing, 23–24, 117–118
Staff
  as customers, 71
  empowering, 12
Staff attitude. *See also* Quality of service
  protocols for, 127–129, 154–156, 172–174
Staff-patient relationship, 10–11
Swearing, patient. *See* Verbally abusive patients
System abusers, 97–100
System problems, 11–12, 89

T

TARP (technical assistance research project), 6,
      9, 22
Telephone, protocols for, 137–138
Threats, against staff, 114–115
3M Corporation, 9
Timeliness, of resolution, 77–78, 79
TQM (total quality management), 2, 5, 11
Tracking, of problems, 10, 11
Training, for service recovery, 10, 12–13
Trending
  in non-physician complaints, 92
  in physician complaints, 85–89
Triage table, for service recovery, 24

V

Value-added component, 18, 32
Verbally abusive patients, 107–111
Violence, workplace, 116–119

W

Word-of-mouth, reputation, 4

Z

Zeithaml, Valarie A., *Delivering Quality Service:
      Balancing Customer Perceptions and
      Expectations*, 3–4
Zemke, Ron, 9, 12, 14, 21, 22
Zero defections, 5. *See also* Loyalty, customer
Zero defects theory, 2
Zone approach to decision making, 12–13

About the Author

Liz Osborne, M.S., has 14 years of experience as manager of a patient relations department for a large HMO using staff model, primary care network and contracted care delivery systems. Ms. Osborne is past president of the Washington Society of Patient Representatives, and is a Fellow and past member of the Board of Directors of the Society for Healthcare Consumer Advocacy. She has spoken at state and national conferences and has taught consumer education classes.

Ms. Osborne has a Bachelor of Arts degree in English Literature from Seattle University and a Master of Science degree in Health-Related Behavior from the University of Washington.

She is affiliated with Sage Consulting, a Novato, CA, consulting firm specializing in organizational development and transformation to increase customer, employee, and physician satisfaction. For more information, contact Sage Consulting, 77 Blanca Drive, Novato, CA, 94947 or go to <www.sageteam.com>.